CREATING A LEARNING ORGANIZATION
Promoting Excellence Through Education

Barbara J. Braham

A FIFTY-MINUTE™ SERIES BOOK

CRISP PUBLICATIONS, INC.
Menlo Park, California

CREATING A LEARNING ORGANIZATION
Promoting Excellence Through Education

Barbara J. Braham

CREDITS
Managing Editor: **Kathleen Barcos**
Editor: **Carol Henry**
Typesetting: **ExecuStaff**
Cover Design: **Carol Harris**
Artwork: **Ralph Mapson**

Copyright © 1995 by Crisp Publications, Inc.

Printed in the United States of America by Bawden Printing Company.

Distribution to the U.S. Trade:

National Book Network, Inc.
4720 Boston Way
Lanham, MD 20706
1-800-462-6420

Library of Congress Catalog Card Number 95-68290
Braham, Barbara J.
Creating a Learning Organization
ISBN 1-56052-351-4

This book is printed on recyclable paper with soy ink.

ABOUT THIS BOOK

Creating a Learning Organization is not like most books. It has a unique "self-paced" format that encourages a reader to become personally involved. Designed to be "read with a pencil," there are exercises, activities, assessments and cases that invite participation.

Learning is one of the few competitive advantages available today. This book gives you the tools to assess if your organization is a learning organization. You'll discover how to get out of the way of learning, and how to support the natural desire in each person to become a lifelong learner.

Creating a Learning Organization can be used effectively in a number of ways. Here are some possibilities:

▶ **Individual Study.** Because the book is self-instructional, all that is needed is a quiet place, some time and a pencil. Completing the activities and exercises will provide valuable feedback, as well as practical ideas for improving your business.

▶ **Workshops and Seminars.** This book is ideal for use during, or as preassigned reading prior to, a workshop or seminar. With the basics in hand, the quality of participation will improve. More time can be spent practicing concept extensions and applications during the program.

▶ **College Programs.** Thanks to the format, brevity and low cost, this book is ideal for short courses and extension programs.

There are other possibilities that depend on the objectives of the user. One thing is certain: Even after it has been read, this book will serve as excellent reference material that can be easily reviewed.

PREFACE

Many organizations today are living with the question, "What is a learning organization?" They're turning the question this way and that, reflecting on it, discussing it, feeling challenged and discouraged by it. More important than the answer to the question, is the fact that the question is being asked. *The question is the answer.* Whenever you encounter a question that grabs you and doesn't seem to want to let go, that is a signal that you have begun a journey, a quest. You might say that's precisely what the word question implies: Quest-I-On.

Creating a Learning Organization is written for people who wonder how to help an organization become a learning organization. If you're living with that question, this book is for you. To become a learning organization, you need to help both the individual and the organization learn, and in this book you will find guidance for those tasks. I hope that along the way it will provoke more questions, as well.

Barbara J. Braham

ABOUT THE AUTHOR

Barbara J. Braham, M.S.W., is a professional speaker and author specializing in personal development for professional success. For the past ten years she has worked with corporations and associations across the country who believe that their people are their greatest asset. Her programs are designed to assist individuals in aligning their personal purpose with the organizational purpose. In addition, she helps organizations secure their futures by developing the capacity of their people to become lifelong learners.

She offers a variety of in-depth personal retreats for individuals committed to deepening themselves personally and professionally. For information about her services, or to give her feedback about this book, please call or write:

Barbara Braham
1143 Neil Avenue
Columbus, OH 43201
(614) 291–0155

ACKNOWLEDGMENTS

A special thanks to the following people for their contribution to the manuscript: Bill Bickham, Harry Buntyn, Eric Burkland, Leslie Charles, Jeff Douglas, Bill Keller, Valerie Lenart, Susan Schubert, Rick Sullivan, Bill Wienhoff and my Speakers Circle.

This book is dedicated to all who aspire to deeply know themselves.

CONTENTS

P A R T

I

Why Become a Learning Organization?

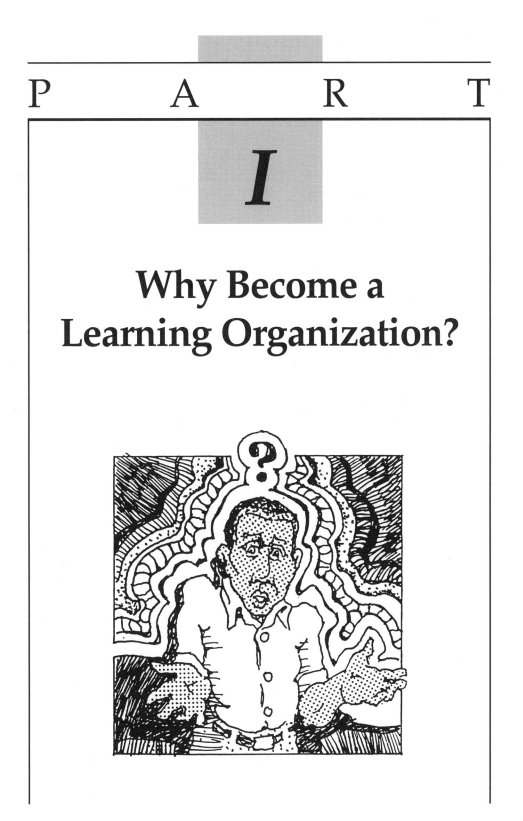

LEARNING ORGANIZATION CHECKLIST

Complete the following checklist. Place a ✓ in front of each statement that is true for your organization to determine the current learning climate. Give an example of the statements you checked in the space provided.

☐ **1.** Learning is integrated into everything people do.

_____

☐ **2.** Learning for learning's sake is encouraged and often rewarded.

_____

☐ **3.** Our organization strongly supports teamwork, creativity, empowerment and quality.

_____

☐ **4.** Employees are trusted to choose the courses that they need.

_____

☐ **5.** People with different job titles from different departments learn together.

_____

☐ **6.** We promote mentoring relationships to enhance learning.

_____

☐ **7.** Learning is integrated into meetings, work groups and work processes.

_____

☐ **8.** All individuals, regardless of position, have equal access to learning.

_____

☐ **9.** We treat mistakes as learning opportunities.

_____

☐ **10.** We have initiated cross-training and reward employees who learn a wider range of job skills.

_____

It is hoped that you were able to put a checkmark in each box, as each of the 10 items are found in true learning organizations. However, if you have items without checkmarks, congratulations, you have just learned that your organization has areas that need development. And that is what this book is all about!

WHAT IS A LEARNING ORGANIZATION?

> *A learning organization is an organization that prioritizes learning.*

Learning is simultaneously both a process and a value. Ideally, every individual in the company, regardless of position or tenure, is committed to being better tomorrow than they are today—through learning. The organization as a whole is committed to continual improvement of every facet of itself, its products and its services—by learning about learning. As both the individual and the organization develop, employees will feel a renewed connection to their work, customers will be better served and the organization will create a future for itself.

A learning organization is set apart from other organizations in these ways:

► Learning is integrated into everything people do; it's a regular part of the job, not "something extra" you add on.

► Learning is a process, not an event.

► Cooperation is the foundation of all relationships.

► Individuals themselves evolve and grow, and in the process transform the organization.

► The learning organization is creative; individuals co-create the organization.

► The organization learns from itself; employees teach the organization about efficiency, quality improvement and innovation.

► It is fun and exciting to be part of a learning organization.

In the learning organization, motivation is recognized as being inherent in each person. With a shared vision and commitment to that vision, people will motivate themselves to learn. Rather than being threatened to learn, it's assumed that individuals and teams will proactively set their own learning agendas. Initially, the organization may need to provide resources and coaching to help people learn how to do this.

There are two significant differences between the content of learning inside a learning organization and the content of learning in other organizations.

1. Employees in a learning organization learn about the business side of their company. They have access to more information than ever before on sales goals, marketing plans and financial statements. In a learning organization, this information is no longer for management or executive eyes only. With employees empowered to make more decisions, they need to understand those decisions in the overall context of the business.

2. Individuals learn how to use their own selves as tools. Never before has this been so important. The learning organization has discovered that "soft is hard." In other words, interpersonal skills, creativity, responsiveness to change and learning how to learn are the skills that serve a person and therefore the organization in the global marketplace of the 1990s. The learning organization needs individuals capable of managing themselves; people who understand that the skill with which they manage themselves will determine how others respond to them. Technical skill alone will not guarantee success.

Communication in the learning organization has taken a quantum leap—one that is both frightening and exciting. Today the purpose of communication goes beyond speaking clearly; communication is now attempting to create community. In such an environment, honesty, self-awareness, cooperation and acceptance are the staples. Communication of such depth facilitates learning, about oneself and about the work. For perhaps the first time, it is not necessary to erect a barrier between who you are on the job and who you are at home.

- You can bring your whole self to work

- You are enriched

- Your work is enriched

- Everyone learns

WHAT IS A LEARNING ORGANIZATION?
(continued)

The Organization's New Direction

The learning organization perceives itself as a living system. Every part is connected to every other part. As in a living organism, there is enormous pressure to maintain homeostasis: If you try to change one part, other parts of the system will make a concerted effort to restore the status quo. Once change has in fact occurred, however, it will affect the entire system. *Systems thinking* allows the organization to focus on *systems change*, rather than searching for one guilty party when there's a problem.

What does a learning organization learn? Everything. However, most organizations begin by focusing on one of these areas:

- ► work products

- ► work processes

- ► teamwork

- ► customers

- ► systems thinking

- ► mental models

QUIZ: *True or False*

Your organization may already be well on its way toward becoming a learning organization, or this may be your first introduction to the concept. Take the following true/false quiz to get a better understanding of how your organization responds to the learning needs of employees.

	TRUE	FALSE
We work to remove barriers to learning.	☐	☐
We cultivate a "learner friendly" environment.	☐	☐
We identify tools our organization can use to become a learning organization.	☐	☐
We understand how adults learn and use that knowledge to our advantage.	☐	☐
We use various tools to assess employees' learning progress.	☐	☐
We acknowledge that people learn from experience.	☐	☐
We recognize what type of learning is most appropriate for our situation.	☐	☐
We encourage each employee to become a lifelong learner.	☐	☐
We encourage employees to keep an open mind to learning.	☐	☐
We understand the factors that inhibit learning.	☐	☐
We know how to motivate people to learn.	☐	☐

Any statement marked false represents an area that needs to be developed as you create a learning organization.

WHY IS LEARNING SO IMPORTANT NOW?

Things are changing so fast today that it is difficult to keep up with the pace. People who can't keep up with those changes may find themselves "downsized" or "rightsized"—or some other euphemism for *out of work*. A business that can't change in tune with the global marketplace probably has no future.

YOU CAN'T SLOW DOWN CHANGE

THERE IS NOWHERE TO HIDE

NO INDUSTRY IS IMMUNE

What's the answer? The answer is *learning*.

It is one of the few, if not the only competitive advantage available today. Moreover, it is the healthiest response in a world of rapid change. The question is no longer *if* you will use available technology, from voice mail to computers, of *if* you will use the business technologies of problem solving, meeting facilitation and teamwork. The question today is how quickly, how efficiently, and how effectively can the people in your organization become proficient in using the technologies.

Organizations and individuals that are able to learn with the greatest ease and speed will be the most successful in the future. Today a person cannot expect the current level of knowledge and expertise to serve him or her for years down the road. That assumption will result in unemployment and disillusionment. With knowledge and technology advancing so quickly, you don't have years to "get up to speed." The secret, then, is identifying the need to learn, and then setting yourself to the task quickly and efficiently.

Learning is not the same thing as acquiring knowledge any more than data is the same as information. When you learn, your behavior changes. As Peter Senge wrote in *The Fifth Discipline*,

> Real learning gets to the heart of what it means to be human. Through learning we re-create ourselves. Through learning we become able to do something we never were able to do. Through learning we reperceive the world and our relationship to it. Through learning we extend our capacity to create, to be part of the generative process of life. There is within each of us a deep hunger for this type of learning.*

Senge is right—there is a deep hunger for learning. It is painful for individuals to stand by and watch their company inhibit learning. It is frustrating when employees can't apply what they know. It is discouraging when the organization makes unnecessary mistakes. Standing by and watching this happen will damage people's spirits. Creating a learning organization can restore that spirit to "respirit" the workplace.

EXERCISE AHEAD

---

* Peter Senge, *The Fifth Discipline*, New York: Doubleday, 1992, p. 14.

EXERCISE: Why Your Organization Might Want to Be a Learning Organization

Check all the reasons why your organization might want to pursue becoming a learning organization. Add your own reasons if they're not listed.

- ☐ To stay in business
- ☐ To remain competitive
- ☐ To be a leader in your field or industry
- ☐ To better serve the needs of your customers/clients/patients
- ☐ To increase profitability
- ☐ To be a role model for your suppliers
- ☐ To prevent mistakes
- ☐ To avoid repeating mistakes
- ☐ To benefit from all the gifts your employees have to contribute
- ☐ To raise the organization's collective I.Q.
- ☐ To create a motivating work environment
- ☐ To attract and retain outstanding employees
- ☐ To build on the organization's strengths and to leverage previous successes
- ☐ To support the growth and development of your employees
- ☐ To "respirit" the workplace
- ☐ To contribute new products/knowledge/services to the world
- ☐ To become better at what you do
- ☐ To implement your Total Quality Management program
- ☐ To sustain your Total Quality Management program
- ☐ To help employees learn how to work together more effectively
- ☐ _____
- ☐ _____

WHAT'S THE INVESTMENT?

Having anything of value requires an initial investment from you. If you want good health, you need to exercise, eat right, maintain a positive attitude and get adequate rest.

What It Will Take

TIME

If you want employees to commit themselves to learning, learning needs to be part of the regular workday—not an add-on or an afterthought. Don't expect employees to prove their commitment to learning by doing it on their own time. Certainly they may give their own time, but if you want yours to be a learning organization, then your commitment is to allocate time for learning. How much time is enough? It will vary depending upon your industry and each person's specific role. In general, though, think about allocating 10% of the work week. Yes, that's four hours every week dedicated to learning. You'll find that you'll recoup that time, however, in the elimination of wasted effort, duplication and bureaucratic confusion.

MONEY

Expect to spend money on training, training materials, time away from the job while learning, and on hiring internal and external experts. What percentage of your organization's payroll is allocated to training? The United States industry average is 1.2%. A minimum recommended standard is 2%, and 4% if you're serious about becoming a learning organization. Motorola invested 1.5% in 1985; it saw such a return on its investment that by 1994 its commitment was up to 4%.*

COMMUNICATION

Employees need to understand why learning is important. There will also be an intensified need to keep people informed so that learning is conveyed from one part of the company to another.

Business Week, March 28, 1994, pp. 158–163.

WHAT'S THE INVESTMENT? (continued)

What It Will Do

PRODUCE CHANGE

Not all of the changes will be easy or fun. You may discover habits in yourself or traditions in your organization that need to be changed. It will often be unclear initially whether the changes are beneficial. With change may come stress, and you can expect resistance to the changes. As individuals learn, however, they'll put pressure on the organization to change.

TEST YOUR ABILITY TO FIND BALANCE

It is challenging for an organization to pursue learning simultaneously while getting its usual work done. Too much focus on the process of learning, and the business slips; too little focus on learning, and the business slips. The point of balance is often elusive. Clarity of purpose is essential.

What investments will be easiest for your organization to make?

_____

_____

Which ones will be most difficult?

_____

_____

Business   Learning

WHO'S RESPONSIBLE FOR LEARNING?

Both the organization and its individuals have a responsibility for learning. But for each of them, the responsibilities are different.

The organization is responsible for providing learning opportunities and a structure that supports learning. Equally important, it needs to remove barriers to learning—learn how to get out of the way!

Even the best-designed learning structure, however, cannot *make* someone learn. The individuals within the organization will need to use the opportunities made available to them. It is the individual who is responsible for translating knowledge into learning on a day-to-day basis.

When your company supports learning, it makes it easier for individual employees to learn. But even if learning is not a priority within an organization, that does not absolve the individuals of their learning responsibilities. Each day, each experience, can be a learning experiment.

Take a moment now to think through your personal responsibility for and commitment to learning.

Why is learning important to you?

_____

_____

In what ways are you committed to learning?

_____

_____

What is your perception of your organization's commitment to learning?

_____

_____

Why do you believe learning is important to your company at this time?

_____

_____

P A R T

II

What It Takes to Become a Learning Organization

TOOLS IMPORTANT TO A LEARNING ORGANIZATION

As Peter Senge said in *The Fifth Discipline*, becoming a learning organization is not about emulating a "model." Rather, you create the learning environment as you go, based on your organization, its customers, problems, markets and individual personalities. "Aspiring" learning organizations share many common characteristics, but perhaps the most important is a willingness to continue learning. Remember that no matter how much you learn, there is always more to learn.

In this section we will identify some of the tools your organization can use in its quest to become a learning organization. Many of the tools used by a learning organization are also used by the traditional, hierarchical organization (from now on, we'll call this the *telling organization*). The difference is in why the tools are used, who uses them, and when and where they are used. Before we examine those tools, take a look at the following chart. It summarizes the differences, in terms of learning characteristics, between learning in the telling organization and the learning organization.

TOOLS IMPORTANT TO A LEARNING ORGANIZATION (continued)

Learning Characteristic	Telling Organization	Learning Organization
Who Learns?	People Who Are: "Sent"; Rewarded; or Related Groups (i.e., Managers or Sales People)	Everyone: All employees; All Departments and Levels
Who Teaches?	In-house Trainers or Outside Experts	People Closest to the Work, Trainers, Some "Experts"
Who's Responsible?	Training Department	Everyone
What Learning Tools Do People Use?	Courses, On-the-Job Training (OTJ), Mentoring, Formal Training, Learning Plans	Courses, OTJ Training, Learning Plans, Mentors, Benchmarks, Teams, Personal Reflection, Partnerships
When Do People Learn?	When Required, First Few Months on Job, As Needed	All the Time, For Long Term
What Skills Do They Learn?	Technical	Technical, Business, Interpersonal, How to Learn
Where Do They Learn?	Classes, On the Job	Classes, Meetings, Doing the Work, Everywhere
Time	Today's Needs	Future Needs
Feeling	Soulless	Spirited

Many organizations are confused by the "how"—the tools—of learning. They mistakenly think that if they offer courses and have a tuition reimbursement program, that makes them a learning organization. But the tools, as you can see from the chart, are not what separates a learning organization from a telling organization. The tools are like bricks; you can use them to build a cathedral or a prison.

THE TOOLS AND THEIR CONTINUUMS

Now let's explore each of the learning tools and how they are used differently by a telling and learning organization. Each tool is set up on a *continuum*. At the far left end of the continuum are indications of how the tool is used in a telling organization, symbolized with a pyramid (△). The telling organization is characterized by control, competitiveness, short-term quantitative results, reactiveness and functional units that operate in silos (isolated units). The telling organization "works hard." In your company today, this may be how one or more of these tools are being used.

At the right end of the continuum are indications of how the tool is used by organizations consciously trying to become learning organizations, symbolized by a circle (○). These organizations are characterized by:

✔ TEAMWORK

✔ COOPERATION

✔ CREATIVITY

✔ EMPOWERMENT

✔ QUALITY

The learning organization "works smart." You may recognize your organization at this end of the continuum, or perhaps you're somewhere in the middle.

As you read through each tool's description, mark the point on the continuum where you would place your organization today, with the date. You may place your company all the way to the left, the right or somewhere in between. Remember, this is an assessment tool, not a judgment tool.

Return to these continuums every six months. Notice where your organization makes changes, and move your organization forward or backward accordingly. You may even discover that your company has moved beyond the right end of the continuum.

Continuum #1: Tuition Reimbursement

Place an *X* on the line to mark where your organization is today, and date it.

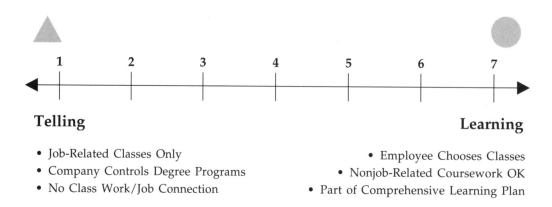

Telling

- Job-Related Classes Only
- Company Controls Degree Programs
- No Class Work/Job Connection

Learning

- Employee Chooses Classes
- Nonjob-Related Coursework OK
- Part of Comprehensive Learning Plan

Many companies have a tuition-reimbursement program. According to the program, an employee can attend certain preapproved courses that are directly related to the job or are part of the requirements for a degree related to the job. To be reimbursed, the employee may be required to earn a certain grade or commit to a specified number of years of service. Rarely is any application made of the classroom learning to actual on-the-job tasks.

Companies moving toward the right end of the continuum will reimburse tuition for classes that are job-related as well as classes that aren't. For example, your company might pay for a secretary to take accounting courses. Most important, the learning organization consciously seeks to integrate the classroom experience with the job. Sometimes partners or teams go to classes together to increase the on-the-job application. Other times, the integration takes place through conversation, using questions such as these:

▶ What are you learning?

▶ How can you apply it in this work setting?

▶ What questions does it provoke about how your work is being done?

▶ Can you complete any class projects using a real-life job situation?

1. What is your company's current policy regarding tuition reimbursement?

_____

_____

2. How many times have you taken advantage of this program?

_____

_____

3. How many people in your department use tuition reimbursement?

_____

_____

4. What is in place to guide course selection?

_____

_____

Continuum #2: Formal Training

Place an X on the line to mark where your organization is today.

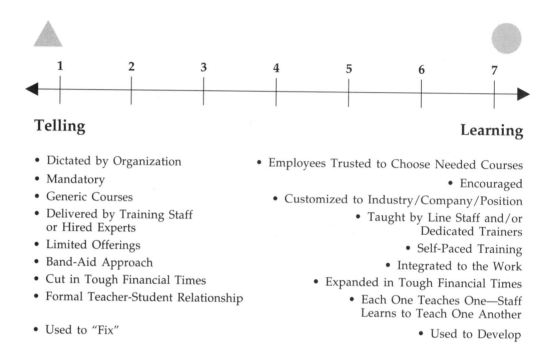

Telling   **Learning**

- Dictated by Organization
- Mandatory
- Generic Courses
- Delivered by Training Staff or Hired Experts
- Limited Offerings
- Band-Aid Approach
- Cut in Tough Financial Times
- Formal Teacher-Student Relationship

- Used to "Fix"

- Employees Trusted to Choose Needed Courses
- Encouraged
- Customized to Industry/Company/Position
- Taught by Line Staff and/or Dedicated Trainers
- Self-Paced Training
- Integrated to the Work
- Expanded in Tough Financial Times
- Each One Teaches One—Staff Learns to Teach One Another
- Used to Develop

In the telling organization, learning is like ice, rigid and frozen. Although both the training department and individuals feel that they're "chipping away" at learning, it still remains a solid block that sits in the training department most of the time. When the block is sent to a department, it gets put on a shelf where it silently watches, not participating. Or individuals may attend a training program and return excited about implementing a new idea, only to be told, "That's not the way we do things here." When there's a problem, one of the first solutions is to "throw training at it." In this environment—with training on the left end of the continuum—the risk is that while some individuals may learn, the organization does not learn.

Contrast this with the learning organization, where learning flows like a river through every department and location doing its work. As it moves from one department to another, it is enriched and carries along much more than what it started with. Learning flourishes in the flowing river. The learning is integrated everywhere, and the organization grows.

In the learning organization, then, training is less an event and more of a process. Everyone gets involved not just in learning, but also in teaching. People learn from one another, and the organization learns from its employees, suppliers, vendors and customers. Instead of homogeneous training classes (managers with managers, secretaries with secretaries), learning groups have diversity in both job title and responsibility. In this environment, learning is not just a one way street. Training is customized to meet the needs of specific groups and projects, rather than expecting the learners to adapt the training to their situation.

In telling organizations, training is an event that takes place when times are good. It is often for select groups of employees, perhaps salespeople or managers. It may even be perceived as either a perk or a punishment. You "get" to go, or you're required to go. There isn't room for *wanting* to go. Consequently, when learning occurs, it is in isolated pockets around the organization.

This changes in a learning organization. No longer are learning events segregated into elite pockets of the company. Learning can happen anytime, anywhere, with anyone. It becomes the responsibility of each person, not just the "training department." Knowledge flows both ways, and individuals continue to learn from the company while the company also learns from its employees.

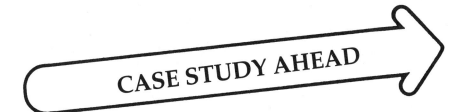

CASE STUDY AHEAD

CONTINUUM #2: FORMAL TRAINING (continued)

CASE STUDY: Becoming a Learning Company

Pier 1 imports, a 32-year-old importer of unique merchandise, is one example of a company whose training has moved from the left to the right end of the continuum. As other retailers began to carry merchandise similar to Pier 1's, it became increasingly difficult for Pier 1 to distinguish itself in the marketplace. After doing some customer surveys, the company decided to increase its selling and service expertise.

The first step was a Crisp Custom Training video-book program on Quality Customer Service. Although a customized product, the program was used as an "event" to fix a problem, not as part of an integrated, graduated, usable program.

Next, Pier 1 worked with an outside company to design a customized selling program. This time the program was attended and supported by all the executives before it was delivered to store managers across 25 regions by an interdisciplinary team. The program signified a shift of focus from merchandise to selling and servicing. Once the managers had been trained, assistant managers were trained. These managers and assistant managers became the training force that introduced 10,000 associates to the new skills and the new focus. Thus the training program has shifted from an event championed by the training department to a process integrated and owned by everyone—from senior executives to individual associates.

Most recently, the Pier 1 training department is compiling a video newsletter to support ongoing training. In many ways the newsletter looks similar to Pier 1's first Crisp video-book program. The difference is that today learning is integrated into the company, and everyone owns the program (not just the training department). Rather than mastery of a particular set of skills, the goal is continuous improvement of selling and servicing skills. Pier 1 continues to move toward the right end of the continuum.

EXERCISE: *Your Training Options*

Training comes in many packages. Place a checkmark in the box by each one that your organization uses.

☐ Internally developed programs

☐ "Off the shelf." In other words, the company purchases a prepared program, often with leaders' guides to help your in-house trainers use it.

☐ Hire outside experts

☐ Public seminars that come through town

☐ Off-site executive programs

☐ Customized books

☐ Customized videos

☐ CBT (computer-based training)

☐ CAI (computer-aided instruction)

☐ Satellite programs

☐ Off-the-shelf audio or video learning programs

Continuum #3: Mentoring

Place an X on the line to mark where your organization is today, and date it.

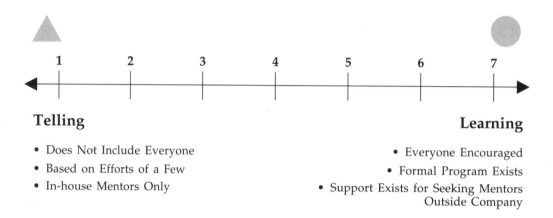

Telling
- Does Not Include Everyone
- Based on Efforts of a Few
- In-house Mentors Only

Learning
- Everyone Encouraged
- Formal Program Exists
- Support Exists for Seeking Mentors Outside Company

In the hierarchical organization, someone with position and status becomes the mentor, offering a helping hand through project assistance, advice, networking and political support to a bright, talented up-and-comer in the company. The mentoring relationship thus becomes a significant source of learning for the younger, less-experienced person. As a result, his or her career often progresses faster than the norm.

In a learning organization, these relationships aren't left to chance. Individuals are actively recruited to mentor, and others are selected to be mentored. No one is left out of the process. Mentoring is used less for advancing someone's career than for advancing the learning process. Learning organizations recognize that in a successful mentoring relationship, the mentor learns as much as the "mentee." The content of mentoring goes beyond political and technical skills to the essence of how to learn. Additionally, mentoring can become a significant tool in creating the shared values of a learning culture.

How does mentoring occur in your company?

_____

_____

How could mentoring help your organization become a learning organization?

_____

_____

Continuum #4: On-the-Job (OTJ) Training

Place an *X* on the line to mark where your organization is today, and date it.

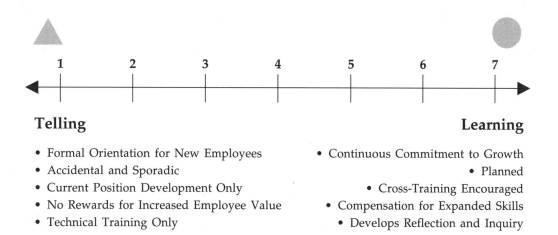

Telling   **Learning**

- Formal Orientation for New Employees
- Accidental and Sporadic
- Current Position Development Only
- No Rewards for Increased Employee Value
- Technical Training Only

- Continuous Commitment to Growth
- Planned
- Cross-Training Encouraged
- Compensation for Expanded Skills
- Develops Reflection and Inquiry

On the left end of the continuum, on-the-job (OTJ) training is confined to orientation and technical training. Individuals usually receive this type of learning experience in the first few months of employment. If a new piece of equipment or technology is introduced, there may be another period of training to get people "up and running."

As the organization moves toward the right end of the continuum, learning becomes fully integrated into the culture of the company and is valued for itself. Learning is integrated into meetings, work products and work processes. Time is routinely set aside to assess the learning from any given experience. Teams of people get together not just to solve problems or learn from mistakes, but to celebrate and learn from successes.

Cross-training—learning other jobs within the department or the company—is an element of OTJ training that is supported in learning organizations.* It is often reinforced by the company by awarding higher pay to those who have learned more job skills. Cross-training increases the organization's capacity to respond to changing customer needs. It provides the individual an opportunity to continue growing.

---

* This may be limited in some organizations by labor contracts.

CONTINUUM #4: ON-THE-JOB (OTJ) TRAINING (continued)

OTJ learning is not limited just to technical skills, either. Reflection and inquiry, two interpersonal skills (known as "soft" skills), are examples of the new ways OTJ training is being used today in learning organizations. Every aspect of the job becomes a potential opportunity for learning to use these skills.

CASE STUDY: Time for Reflection

At the Ohio Manufacturers' Association, for example, reflection is integrated into their meetings. At the beginning of a meeting, meeting participants are asked about what they've reflected on since the last meeting. This is a chance to raise issues, clarify points from the previous meeting, and share any learning that is relevant. At the close of the meeting, another five minutes or so are allocated to reflect on how productive the meeting was. This is not a time to rehash the content of the meeting, but rather to comment on how effectively it was run. Is there anything that might be reinforced, strengthened, repeated or deleted at the next meeting to make it more effective? In addition to the benefits of keeping the focus on learning, the reflection process has all but eliminated the "meeting after the meeting" phenomenon.

Briefly describe how your company uses cross-training to enhance productivity and increase employee value to the company.

_____

_____

Excluding the training you received as a new employee, what on-the-job training have you participated in?

_____

_____

What does your company do to encourage learning at work?

_____

_____

Continuum #5: Staff Development or Learning Plans

Place an *X* on the line to mark where your organization is today, and date it.

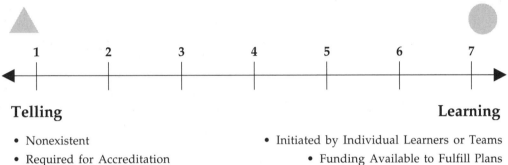

Telling

- Nonexistent
- Required for Accreditation
- Filed and Reviewed Perfunctorily for Annual Reviews

Learning

- Initiated by Individual Learners or Teams
- Funding Available to Fulfill Plans
- Monitored by Individual Learners

On the left end of the continuum, staff development plans (when they exist) are instruments of control. Some organizations—hospitals, for instance—need these plans to maintain accreditation, and therefore they become a required part of the annual review process. Employee and manager both dread the process of filling out such development plans, and quickly learn how to take advantage of a few key phrases that sound good and don't mean much.

In moving toward the right end of the continuum, the training department may apply pressure on managers and employees to produce development plans. The intent is well-meaning: to have the individual plans provide meaningful data on the overall company training/learning needs. Sadly, both parties typically go through the process in a perfunctory way—the employee not thinking through learning goals; the supervisor identifying broad, vague objectives that can be used generically on all the forms that need to be filled out. In the end, the training department is perceived as creating more work, not as a resource for enhanced performance.

In a true learning organization, the learning plan is an important document to everyone concerned. The individual assumes responsibility for his or her learning and creates a realistic written plan. The organization budgets financial and time resources to support the plan. Because the individual understands the strategic vision, the individual learning goals will support the direction in which the organization is moving.

CONTINUUM #5: STAFF DEVELOPMENT OR LEARNING PLANS (continued)

Rather than a document for control, in a learning organization the development plan becomes a tool for empowerment. If someone wants to attend a course in Florida in February, it isn't assumed that he or she is just trying to get a free vacation. There is trust that the proposed course is the best way to meet the identified need. The request of an employee for a specialized course only available in another state would not be denied because management assumed the employee was interested only in the trip. For many employees, such as single parents, the trip may be a true inconvenience and personal strain, yet they volunteer to go knowing the course will meet their learning objectives. In the learning organization, suspiciousness is replaced with trust as the organization approaches the right end of the continuum.

What courses have you been denied because supervisors felt that your choice was not appropriate or relevant to your job?

_____

_____

_____

_____

What positive steps does your organization take to ensure that employee development plans are effective and realistic?

_____

_____

_____

_____

List at least two classes or courses you would like to take and how you feel your organization would benefit.

_____

_____

_____

_____

Continuum #6: Teamwork

Place an X on the line to mark where your organization is today, and date it.

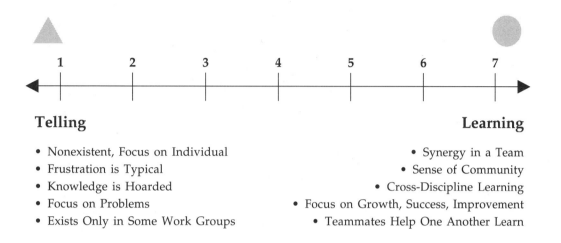

| 1 | 2 | 3 | 4 | 5 | 6 | 7 |

Telling   **Learning**

- Nonexistent, Focus on Individual
- Frustration is Typical
- Knowledge is Hoarded
- Focus on Problems
- Exists Only in Some Work Groups

- Synergy in a Team
- Sense of Community
- Cross-Discipline Learning
- Focus on Growth, Success, Improvement
- Teammates Help One Another Learn

In the telling organization, teamwork is practically nonexistent, or happens by accident. The competitive culture inhibits it. Focus is on individual star performers who compete for training perks. Those who are asked to serve on teams often feel they could do the task faster and more easily by themselves. They've heard about synergy, but they don't usually experience it.

The shift to teamwork (called self-directed teams in some organizations) as the preferred way of doing the work is extremely difficult, because it signifies a shift in the culture, values and norms of the company. The intent is for individuals to learn from one another, or as a team to go outside themselves for the expertise they need. To do this, groups of people need to learn the behaviors that will transform them into a team. These include problem-solving, facilitation skills, decision making, meeting management, conflict resolution, dialog, inquiry and reflection. Team building is a step toward team learning, but does not yet describe a learning organization.

Until cooperation replaces competition, shared learning is extremely difficult.

CONTINUUM #6: TEAMWORK (continued)

Not surprisingly, team learning is the exception rather than the norm. In fact, many more companies are praising the benefits of teams than are creating real-life teams. In an effort to facilitate the transition to more teams, and potentially team learning, many experiments are being conducted. Here are just two.

#1 A trainer and consultant in Columbus, Ohio, is changing the focus and methods used by teams. She is blending problem solving with studying achievements by creating success-oriented teams. Learning is enhanced through studying achievements, not just failures.

#2 A consultant in St. Petersburg, Florida, has created Esteem Teams. These are groups of people within companies that are committed to personal learning and development. They get together on a weekly basis and use an audio program as the basis of their learning and development. Each week a different group member leads the discussion. The purpose is to leverage their personal learning toward organizational learning.

Describe how teamwork is being used in your company.

_____

_____

_____

_____

Give an example of team learning that you've observed or experienced.

_____

_____

_____

_____

List some of the successes your teams have experienced.

_____

_____

_____

_____

Continuum #7: Benchmarking

Place an X on the line to mark where your organization is today, and date it.

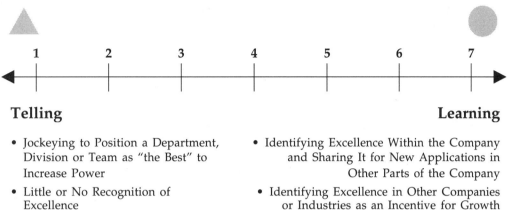

Telling   **Learning**

- Jockeying to Position a Department, Division or Team as "the Best" to Increase Power
- Little or No Recognition of Excellence

- Identifying Excellence Within the Company and Sharing It for New Applications in Other Parts of the Company
- Identifying Excellence in Other Companies or Industries as an Incentive for Growth

On the left end of the continuum, benchmarking (if it is used at all) is a tool of control, used to force a department to increase their productivity or effectiveness.

In a learning organization, the benchmarking process helps teams or work groups look outside themselves to identify learning opportunities. To establish benchmarks, a team identifies another company in the industry or another team in the company, that is perceived to be outstanding at what they do. Then the team studies that organization/team, perhaps making on-site visits and doing interviews with key individuals. Based on the data collected, the team looks for ways to learn from the other company/team's experience, and in the process how they can advance their own team.

Wausau Insurance Company is an example of one company that is using benchmarking to increase its performance. Project leader and internal consultant Ron Laconi has said, "While it's good to compare ourselves from within . . . we also need to look at our competitors who have a reputation as being the best within the insurance industry. For example, we want people to be as satisfied with our billing process as they are with American Express, because American Express has consistently demonstrated its leadership in this area."*

---

* Ford, Susan. "You Can Teach an Old Dog New Tricks." *Good People.* Employers Insurance of Wausau: Wausau, Wisconsin, November 1994, p. 5.

Continuum #8: Partnership

Place an X on the line to mark where your organization is today, and date it.

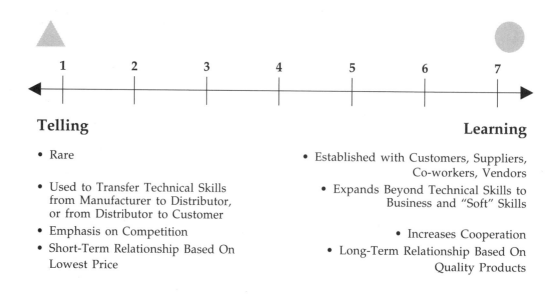

Telling

- Rare

- Used to Transfer Technical Skills from Manufacturer to Distributor, or from Distributor to Customer
- Emphasis on Competition
- Short-Term Relationship Based On Lowest Price

Learning

- Established with Customers, Suppliers, Co-workers, Vendors
- Expands Beyond Technical Skills to Business and "Soft" Skills
- Increases Cooperation
- Long-Term Relationship Based On Quality Products

Until recently, the concept of partnership hasn't been understood outside of a legal agreement or personal relationship. The learning organization recognizes partnership as a significant point of leverage in learning and long-term success. Today there are partnerships with customers, suppliers and even competitors.

CASE STUDY: *Creating A Learning Partnership*

General Electric Appliances is one example of a company that has created a learning partnership with its customers. General Electric produces major appliances that are sold to retail appliance dealers, who then make them available to individual consumers.

In 1992, the company decided to learn more about the world through the eyes of its distributors, and discovered that many of their dealers were small "mom and pop" operations struggling to survive. Armed with this information, General Electric Appliances set out to share its learning with its dealers. Through Crisp Custom Training, the firm produced a book for its dealers, titled *Major Appliance Retailing*. The book is designed to help retailers run their small businesses more successfully.

It proved to be the first step in an ongoing learning partnership. What used to be a we/they relationship has become one of working together to achieve mutual goals. Now many of the retailers are consulting with a General Electric representative to prepare their retail account plans. And as General Electric continues to learn from its customers, the firm gets better at meeting its customers' needs.

EXERCISE AHEAD

EXERCISE: Assess Your Organization

You can assess your overall progress toward becoming a learning organization by adding together your score on each of the tools' continuums. If your total score is 24 or less, you're still functioning primarily as a traditional hierarchical, pyramid organization. A score between 25 and 40 indicates that your organization is in transition. A score of 41 or higher suggests that you've made significant progress toward becoming a learning organization. In the space below, record your score today. Come back at six-month intervals, reassess your organization on each continuum, and note the progress you've made.

	DATE	SCORE	DATE	SCORE	DATE	SCORE
Tuition Reimbursement	___	___	___	___	___	___
Formal Training	___	___	___	___	___	___
Mentoring	___	___	___	___	___	___
OTJ Training	___	___	___	___	___	___
Development/Learning Plans	___	___	___	___	___	___
Teamwork	___	___	___	___	___	___
Benchmarking	___	___	___	___	___	___
Partnership	___	___	___	___	___	___
Total Score	___		___		___	

GETTING—AND KEEPING— THE LEARNING EDGE

If your company is financially strong and morale is positive, it is easy to slip into what we call *learning arrogance.* Obviously, you know how to do things and do them well. Witness your success! But rather than become a learning organization, you may be focused on being a telling organization—telling others how great you are and telling your employees what to do. So why would your business need to learn more, or learn from anyone else?

The reason is, everything changes. Nothing stays constant. And in today's world, the changes are occurring at an amazing speed. In the 1960s, Andy Warhol said we'd each have 15 minutes of fame sometime in our life. Businesses are no exception to this prediction. If your organization is having its moment in the limelight, don't make the mistake of thinking you have arrived. Learn from IBM, Eastern Airlines and Macy's, and remember how fast 15 minutes passes.

When your group is at the peak, that's also the time when you are most vulnerable. Success can blind you. The challenge is to realize that when you've reached a peak, you're really at the crest of a curve, and the next natural move is downward. This is the moment to become proactive and look for the next learning challenge. Take advantage of where you are, and let today's success be the foundation for moving into areas less known. Consider the Microsoft organization: Are they working today on more software packages for computers? No, they're making plans to enter your family room with "edutainment," home shopping and interactive television. Chairman Bill Gates is not letting Microsoft become Learning Arrogant, but is instead keeping his company on their learning edge.

PART

III

The Organization's Responsibility for Learning

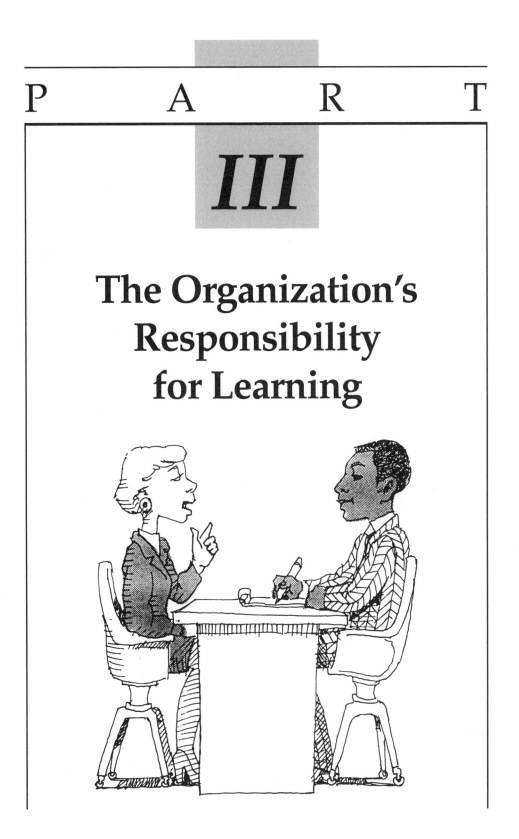

ORGANIZATIONAL ATTITUDES TOWARD LEARNING

Learning is an individual responsibility, yet an organization can go a long way toward providing an environment that supports and encourages individual learning. Young children who have an environment rich in stimuli—colors, shapes, textures, tastes—learn more than children who do not have this environmental support. It is the same for organizations and their adult learners.

Knowing that learning will give the competitive edge in the 1990s and beyond, it's hard to imagine any company not wanting to maximize its support of learning. Here are some of the things that you can do to make your company "learner friendly."

Invest the Time

How much time will you give your employees to learn? If we were talking about money, the typical rule of thumb is to invest 10 percent in your future through savings. That's not a bad guideline for learning, either. Are you willing to invest 10 percent of your employee's time in learning? Ideally, this will happen on a regular, daily basis as opposed to once or twice a year. Why is such regularity so important? It gets employees into the learning habit. As they become oriented to learning in every situation, you can leverage the learning. It becomes cumulative, and takes learning out of the realm of an event and into a regular process.

Include Learning in Your Culture and Values

It's easy to talk about having a commitment to learning, but what of your corporate culture and corporate values? What is really considered important? Do top managers "send employees to training" while staying behind, immersed in their daily tasks? In her seminars, your author has heard many people say, "You know who needs to hear this message? My manager." If training and learning are considered necessary only for the rank and file, and not for everyone, the organization is not sending a message that learning is valued. The opposite condition, too, is detrimental. Consider the following case study on page 42.

ORGANIZATIONAL ATTITUDES TOWARD LEARNING (continued)

CASE STUDY: Learning Is for Everyone

In a recent seminar, a secretary attended along with supervisors and managers. After the program she was filled with enthusiasm. She had worked in the organization eight years, but this was the first training program she had ever attended. She loved the learning and said, "I wish I could go to more programs."

This organization spent training dollars only on its "professional" staff. Unfortunately, this company didn't consider its secretarial staff as professional, and was losing the commitment to learning it might have received from its "nonprofessional" staff.

Review

Take a few minutes now to jot down your organization's values about learning and training.

_____

_____

Are learning opportunities provided for everyone, or only a special group?

_____

_____

Do all individuals have equal access to learning? What are the opportunities?

_____

_____

Is learning a perk, a punishment or a routine part of the job?

_____

_____

Provide Space for Learning

How are your offices laid out? Do people live in cubicles? Are conversations and meetings held behind closed doors? Where are meetings and projects conducted?

It's difficult to learn about the work of others if you don't regularly see them or the work they're doing. Herman Miller, an office furniture manufacturer, asks prospective customers to describe how their work gets done. Based on the answers to this question, furniture is designed for three different styles of teamwork.

Style #1: Linear Teams

Linear teams perform routine, repetitive tasks that are passed from one person to the next until the process is complete and it moves to the next team. Examples of linear teams are inventory control and loan processing. Although meetings do occur to discuss the work, individuals work independently most of the day at their own desks. There is limited learning outside of technical skills.

Offices are next to each other, so work can be passed from one to the next. There is lots of privacy because work is done independently.

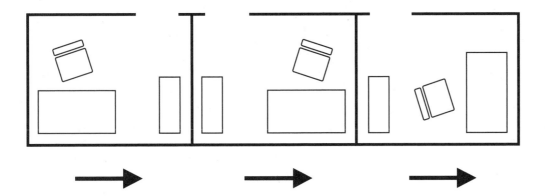

ORGANIZATIONAL ATTITUDES TOWARD LEARNING (continued)

Style #2: Parallel Teams

Parallel teams consist of people with specialized skills essential to achieving project outcomes. Most employees serve on several teams. Parallel teams need meeting space as well as private space. Often, project-related materials need to be kept accessible to all team members. More cross-training and shared knowledge are needed than in a linear team. To facilitate this, the space is designed with many formal and informal meeting spaces, and open offices.

Style #3: Circular Teams

In circular teams, there is the greatest demand for open space and easy communication among team members. Learning is maximized in these democratic teams. Creativity and brainstorming are significant parts of the work, so office spaces use bulletin boards or open walls on which ideas are collected and added to.

According to *The Wall Street Journal*, executives at Aluminum Company of America have recently moved out of their executive suites and into a cluster of cockpit-style offices. The L-shaped desks and tables for small, impromptu meetings have made decision making faster and increased interaction and learning.

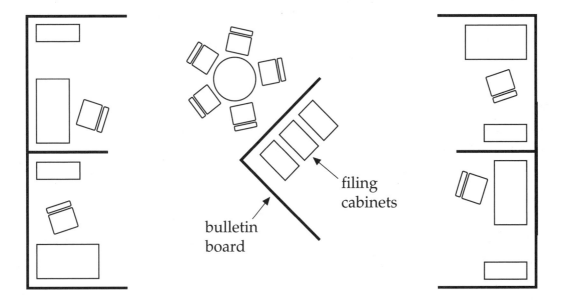

filing
cabinets

bulletin
board

ORGANIZATIONAL ATTITUDES TOWARD LEARNING (continued)

How is your organization using space to facilitate learning?

_____

_____

How does the space promote or inhibit collaboration?

_____

_____

How does the space encourage people to build on the ideas of others?

_____

_____

What physical barriers to learning exist?

_____

_____

How does the space support the current technologies needed to do the work?

_____

_____

How have private offices been configured to encourage informal discussion and problem solving?

_____

_____

Does your physical layout and furniture assume equal access to information, ideas and people?

_____

_____

Respond to Learning Mistakes

In the typical organization, a mistake can result in damage to a person's self-esteem, a lower salary increase or a lost promotion. It is the *atypical* company that treats mistakes as a learning opportunity. In today's environment, businesses need people who are willing to take risks and show initiative. That means errors will be made. How your organization responds to a mistake is crucial, because mistakes can lead to knowledge. Don't sacrifice learning to the expediency of "fixing the mistake," "searching for the guilty" and "damage control." Instead, allow each error to become a learning opportunity.

This isn't to imply that you won't need corrective action following an error. To benefit from the error, however, the organization needs to be willing to stop and reflect on what happened and why.

▶ What can be done differently in the future to prevent the mistake from recurring?

▶ Does the mistake have implications for any other projects or departments in the company?

▶ Who else in the company could benefit from the learning if it were shared?

▶ How have the individuals involved grown as a result of the mistake?

An error says, "Take time for reflection," not, "Make a judgment." With this approach, the company can increase its overall capacity to learn. Stay focused on improving the process, not on looking for someone to blame.

What happens in your company when a mistake is made?

_____

_____

_____

_____

ORGANIZATIONAL ATTITUDES TOWARD LEARNING (continued)

Adopt Proactive versus Retrospective Learning

Learning from mistakes is an example of retrospective learning. In other words, the employee learns something after an event has taken place. Often, the event that provokes the learning is negative—an outright mistake, or perhaps a disappointing or unexpected outcome. Although it's less common, learning from past success is also retrospective learning, and is certainly more motivating.

Unfortunately, with most retrospective learning the essence of what is learned is that the outcome didn't meet expectations or was unpleasant. In these circumstances, people don't necessarily take the next step to change their behavior the next time they are in a similar situation. Further, retrospective learning is by chance. Even if an outcome doesn't meet expectations, that is no guarantee that learning will take place. Perhaps it isn't true that experience is the best teacher!

Something happens ➡ **Maybe you reflect** ➡ **Maybe you learn**

When the learning experience is planned, however, that is the heart of *proactive learning.* In this type of learning, the individual sets a specific and personal learning goal, deciding at the outset what learning is desired. That is not to say some unexpected or unanticipated learning won't occur, but when a plan exists and there is intent to learn, experience is always an excellent teacher. People will miss out on significant learning opportunities when they enter experiences with no plan to learn, and they will leave these experiences without reflecting upon what was gained. Until learning is a focus of attention in every experience, the organization will miss opportunities to integrate and internalize learning into the corporate culture.

Plan to Learn ➡ **Experience** ➡ **You Learn**

Imagine that you are preparing to go to an annual professional conference. How could you plan, proactively, for what you want to learn? Compare your list with the one that follows, which was drawn up by a training director.

_____

_____

_____

_____

_____

_____

_____

What I'll Learn at the Next Annual Conference

○ 1. Networking skills, by meeting with industry people I want to get

to know

2. What training styles are most effective

3. What training technologies are being used by other companies in

my industry

○ 4. How to use humor in my training programs

5. How to select trainers for a program

6. What books other trainers are reading that are influencing their work

7. Industry trends since the last meeting

○ 8. One new idea to help us move toward becoming a learning

organization

ORGANIZATIONAL ATTITUDES TOWARD LEARNING (continued)

Suppose one of the objectives embedded in all your organization's work was, "What can I learn as a result of doing this work?" This mind-set would make everyone a proactive learner. What kind of impact would it make in your company?

Treat Work Like Practice

Work can be an opportunity to practice what you've learned and what you are learning. In fact, many professionals call their work just that, a practice. Physicians have medical practices, lawyers practice law. Therapists and counselors have private practices. The assumption behind this is that they are still learning, still searching for truth. The common thread throughout all of these professions is that learning is the foundation for what they do. The more they practice, the more learning they do, and the better they get. What would happen if people thought of themselves as going to practice each day rather than to work? Would it restore some of the fun and curiosity? Would it reduce the pressure to know it all, or save face by pretending you do?

Reward Employees for Learning

The premise of Michael LeBoeuf's best selling book, *The Greatest Management Principle in the World,* is that behavior that is rewarded is repeated. Why not apply that principle to learning? If you want your employees to be committed to lifelong learning, reward them for learning.

A Learning Quick Check

There are many creative ways to reward employees for learning. In the following list, check the items your company already uses.

☐ Certificates of achievement for classes taken

☐ Articles in the company newsletter about learning experiences

☐ Cash awarded for competencies acquired

☐ Recognition at company-wide meetings

☐ Verbal recognition at the time of learning

☐ Awards given for team learning achievements

☐ Awards given for individual learning achievements

☐ Allocated time at management or team meetings to describe learning experiences

☐ Integration of learning into performance appraisals

☐ _____

☐ _____

BARRIERS TO LEARNING

As much as learning wants to flow through the organization, it often gets dammed up. One of the most important things your organization can do is get out of the way of learning. Actively look for the barriers that inhibit learning or slow it down. Then take steps to remove the obstacles. Here are some of the most common ones.

► **Mixed Messages**

When your organization's words and behavior don't agree, you are sending a mixed message. For example, your company may state a policy that learning is important and may encourage people to attend training. At the same time, however, individuals may still be expected to do their regular work on the days that they attend training. This probably means they have to come in early or work late. It may require that they go back to their desk during lunch, or that when they return from training, the previous day's work is still waiting for them. They're getting a mixed message from your company about the value of learning.

When faced with a mixed message, most people believe the behavior rather than the words. When you send a mixed message about learning, you undermine your objective to become a learning organization.

What mixed messages do you receive? What could be done to improve the situation?

_____

_____

► **Lack of Resources**

Among training and development professionals, it's a widely made assumption that in the face of financial pressures, the first thing to get cut will be training. As you move toward becoming a learning organization, there is no guarantee that your company will not encounter difficult choices in the face of lean times.

What has been your organization's commitment to learning when money is tight?

_____

_____

► Organization Structure

If someone in your company attends a training program or reads a book and is stimulated to try doing things a different way, what happens? Is he or she encouraged to suggest and experiment, or is he or she told, "That's fine for the class or as a theory in a book, but this is the way we do things here"?

Some companies are organized into functional units popularly called silos. In such organizations, the structure itself gets in the way of one functional area's communication with another area. Different departments of the same company may actually pay different prices for the same service from the same vendor. Without a structure that encourages shared learning, learning is isolated to a particular functional unit. The organization pays dearly when learning is localized and not dispersed.

How does your organization ensure that learning is shared across departments?

_____

_____

► Political Environment

In many organizations, power is vested heavily in a few individuals. The rest of the organization spends its energy learning to identify the "pet projects" and key values of those in power. The staff assumes that the more effectively they can play this game, the brighter their career outlook will be. Many employees are consumed by trying to ferret out the desires of those they perceive as powerful. And learning, like any other company objective, may be "on the agenda" or "off the agenda" of those in power.

This political game is acutely visible in government. Newly elected officials may come in with an agenda that may complement or completely undo the previous office holders' work. In one training program offered to a state government agency, employees said that in their 15 years of service, they'd been through six different administrations. The employees' tenure had outlasted all the officials', and the employees continued doing things the way they wanted to do them. Training was endured, not implemented.

BARRIERS TO LEARNING (continued)

Businesses, as well, may be victims of fluctuating priorities, especially with today's rate of change among CEOs and presidents. At a resort, the CEO and president was deeply committed to training and to developing a learning organization. Employees attended many training programs, and had raised expectations of being involved in company decisions and communication. When the resort experienced financial difficulties, a new president was hired—one who focused not on the development of employees, but on the bottom line. Five years later, yet another new president was on the scene, and again committed to training. Not surprisingly, this resort's employees are taking a "wait and see" attitude.

How have politics affected the learning agenda in your organization?

_____

_____

► Unclear, Conflicting, or Missing Vision

A vision provides direction to an organization and its employees. It helps clarify what is important. Without a vision, or with one that is unclear, it is difficult to know what needs to be learned. The organization that tells its employees they are responsible for their learning without giving them a context for that learning does a disservice to those employees. For instance, an art class might be appropriate for someone who will be using desktop publishing in his or her work. If, however, the organization plans to outsource its newsletter and other company publications, that art class may be irrelevant.

In one teaching hospital, the neurology department spent time and money developing a proposed learning program for interns. When they presented their proposal to senior management, the department members were told that their plan didn't fit with the hospital's vision, which was to expand the market for the hospital's services. What do you imagine happened to the neurology department's morale and motivation for learning?

Can you write out the mission and vision of your organization without "looking it up?"

_____

_____

MANAGING ORGANIZATIONAL LEARNING

Perhaps the greatest challenge in creating a learning organization is to see that the learning flows into every nook and cranny of the business. It's one thing to offer courses or send people to seminars, and even to be certain that the training is well delivered and customized to your organization's needs. But how do you manage the actual implementation of the learning? How do you support and facilitate the application of knowledge so that true learning does occur? And how do you make sure this is happening across an organization of diverse people, perhaps diverse locations, among jobs with differing demands and constraints?

In this section, we will attempt to shed some light on these questions.

THREE STYLES OF LEARNING

STYLE #1: Spontaneous Learning

Learning goes on all the time to greater or lesser degrees. Sometimes the learning is *spontaneous* to the project or task at hand. For example, as you're filling a box with product to be sent to a customer, you learn how to pack the box most efficiently. You learn that by the way you place the items in the box, you can increase the number shipped from 18 to 20.

Write an example of spontaneous learning that you've experienced or observed at your company.

_____

_____

STYLE #2: Accidental Learning

Accidental learning occurs as an unexpected outcome of a situation. Imagine you're in a meeting where someone is angry and starts to yell at the chairperson. The chairperson does not appear upset or defensive, but instead calmly reflects the person's feelings, restores control to the meeting and moves on with the agenda. Later, during the same meeting, anger is directed at you. You're surprised to find yourself responding with the same kind of composure the chairperson displayed. You did not go to the meeting planning to learn how to handle an angry person; nor was that the content of the meeting. By accident, you learned this productive way to handle the situation.

Unfortunately, not all accidental learning is positive. Using the previous example, it's just as likely that you could learn to yell right back and attempt to intimidate others when they want something.

List examples of accidental learning that you've experienced or observed.

_____

_____

_____

_____

Passive Learning

In accidental and spontaneous learning, the learner does not make a conscious decision to learn. The learning was not proactive. Rather, it happened unintentionally and was an outcome of experience. This passive approach to learning is how most people say they learn. They think they are learning all the time. Therefore, why put any special attention to learning?

The goal in getting an individual to focus and direct his or her efforts toward learning is to increase the probability that that person will experience spontaneous and accidental learning. When attention is directed to learning, people become more attuned to learning opportunities. They see what was always there but may have been overlooked.

Analogy: Think about the last new car you bought. Like many people, before you bought your car you probably didn't pay much attention to your particular make, model, or color of car on the road. Suddenly, though, after you buy it, you see your new car everywhere!

For individuals to increase their spontaneous and accidental learning, they need to increase their *planned* learning.

$$\boxed{STYLE\ \#3\ Planned\ Learning}$$

In contrast to the other two styles of learning, *planned* learning is conscious. It is a goal purposefully set. It can happen in a classroom or on the job. It can happen with a customer, a vendor, a co-worker or a boss. The critical variable is that learning is the desired outcome. An individual goes into the situation with the intention to learn, to be proactive.

One key to creating a learning organization is to increase the emphasis and commitment to planned learning, rather than trusting that it will happen on its own. When some forethought has been given to what needs to be learned from a situation or experience, learning can occur in nearly any context.

Jot down the ways in which your company currently encourages planned learning.

_____

_____

_____

EXERCISE: *Planned Learning*

Imagine that you work in a social service agency. Some of your routine tasks are listed below. Write down possible learning opportunities that you see in these routine tasks.

To get you started, one possible idea is listed for each task.

TASK: **Attend meetings with community members**

LEARNING:

Learn how to influence community leaders in meetings

_____

_____

TASK: **Be in charge of five major projects**

LEARNING:

Learn how to manage multiple priorities

_____

_____

TASK: **Be an agency spokesperson during times of community crisis**

LEARNING:

Learn how to communicate effectively with the public through the media

_____

_____

TASK: **Supervise a staff of eight**

LEARNING:

Practice giving feedback that is specific

_____

_____

Think about the increased learning potential for your company if, during the hiring process and orientation period, new employees were asked to set learning objectives for the key components of their job. As they gained experience on the job, they could leverage those objectives by sharing them with their work group or team. In this way, learning would become more integrated into the work itself, and not seen as something "extra" to be added on.

What are some of the routines in your job?

_____

_____

_____

What are you learning as you practice these routines?

_____

_____

_____

DETERMINING WHAT TYPE OF LEARNING IS NEEDED

Just as learning can occur in different ways, there are different types of learning. As you improve the opportunities for planned learning to occur, you may begin to consider what type of learning will move your organization most efficiently toward the desired outcomes. In this section we will examine beginner's learning, incremental learning, unlearning, and transformational learning.

First Learning

Perhaps individuals know nothing about what needs to be learned. In this case, you facilitate *first learning*—or what is called *Beginner's Mind* in Zen meditation practice. You invite people to enter the learning experience with an open mind; to have no expectations or preconceived ideas. Shunryu Suzuki says, in *Zen Mind, Beginner's Mind,* "In the beginner's mind there are many possibilities, but in the expert's there are few." Most training programs would be more successful if learners entered the classroom with Beginner's Mind.

Incremental Learning

When you want to build on existing strengths and skills, you need *incremental learning,* in which a skill is refined over time. For example, a manager who gives presentations may be, in general, quite effective. However, the manager could have more impact with a stronger closing statement. Incremental learning for this manager would involve adding to other presentation skills the ability to make concise summaries.

Enhancing or expanding a skill is also incremental learning. For example, consider a group of salespeople who have mastered the selling process. You want them to integrate more customer service after each sale. This is another example of incremental learning.

Unlearning

Increasingly, the task for employees is not to add to what they already know or to learn something new, but to *unlearn* what they know. This is especially true in technological fields. With a new release of a computer program, for example, some incremental learning may be required. But another significant requirement may be to unlearn the old version. For example, a "Print" command key in one version of the program may have been changed to mean "Save to Disk" in the new version. You need to "forget" what you knew in order to be open to remembering the new information.

Many people are reluctant to unlearn what they know. How often have you heard the phrase, "We've always done it this way," or "If it ain't broke, don't fix it"? These phrases reflect a desire to maintain the status quo. In incremental learning, you keep your current learning and body of knowledge and add to it in some way. In unlearning, what you have done and known before becomes obsolete and is dropped to make room for something new.

Zen and the Art of Learning

There is a wonderful Zen story that describes why we sometimes need to empty ourselves first, before we can learn. A university professor went to visit a Zen master at a temple in Japan. As he was seated for tea with the master, the professor began talking. On and on he went, without a pause. As he spoke, the master poured tea. Suddenly the professor jumped up, realizing that the tea had overflowed the cup, the saucer, and was now in his lap. Yet still the master poured. "Stop! What are you doing?!" The master looked up and said, "Just as the cup can hold no more tea when it is full, how can I teach you when your mind is already full?"

DETERMINING WHAT TYPE OF LEARNING IS NEEDED (continued)

Transformational Learning

The last type of learning is called a *paradigm shift* or *transformational learning.* This is the most powerful of all the types of learning, because it shifts a person's point of view on the world. As a consequence, a paradigm shift is often followed by a cascade of unlearning and incremental learning. Some organizations refer to this type of learning as *culture change.*

A paradigm shift is profound and can happen in a flash. There is a moment of "Aha!" when the individual "gets it" and suddenly sees things in a different way. The new paradigm transforms their world view in a significant way. Interestingly enough, a paradigm shift often involves seeing what was previously true as false, or what was false as true.

Here are some examples of paradigm shifts:

► You see your customer instead of your boss as the center of your business.

► Your boss sees his or her job as that of serving you rather than controlling you.

► You become partners with your competitors.

► You change from "having a job" to "doing meaningful work."

► The organization shifts from being a series of functional parts to being an integrated whole.

► The focus of an organization or individual shifts from solving problems to achieving successful solutions.

What paradigm shifts are occurring at your company?

_____

_____

Reflect on the learning that is most needed in your organization at this moment in time. Does it need first learning, incremental learning, unlearning or transformational learning? _____

DEVELOPING RESOURCES—AND RESOURCEFULNESS—IN LEARNING

In a learning organization, the training department is not the primary source of learning experiences or opportunities. That is too narrow and too short-sighted. Instead, the whole body of work, every person in the organization, and every project all become potential sites for learning. Even competitors, suppliers and customers can be resources for learning. The challenge is to *identify and access these learning resources.*

In planned learning, you take time to think through what needs to be learned. From whom or what can it best be learned? What is the time frame in which it needs to be learned? Will a formal educational course be necessary? Is there a book, video, or audio program that will meet the need?

Imagine for a moment that you need to learn the following things. What resources would you tap in your organization?

► How to negotiate with a supplier for a product you need.

Learning resources: _____

► How to resolve a conflict with a co-worker.

Learning resources: _____

► How to write a better business letter.

Learning resources: _____

► How to be less judgmental during meetings.

Learning resources: _____

► How to engage the support of others for a project you're working on.

Learning resources: _____

It may happen that an individual will complain, "My boss is incompetent. I can't learn anything from him/her. I'm stuck in a dead end here." That is a very narrow view, in which the boss is the only learning resource that is identified. Don't let anyone fall into this trap! It's important to help everyone see the full range of learning resources available to them.

Now that we've covered the aspects of your organization's responsibility for creating a climate conducive to learning, we will turn our attention to the responsibilities of an individual for learning and personal mastery.

PART

IV

The Individual's Responsibility for Learning

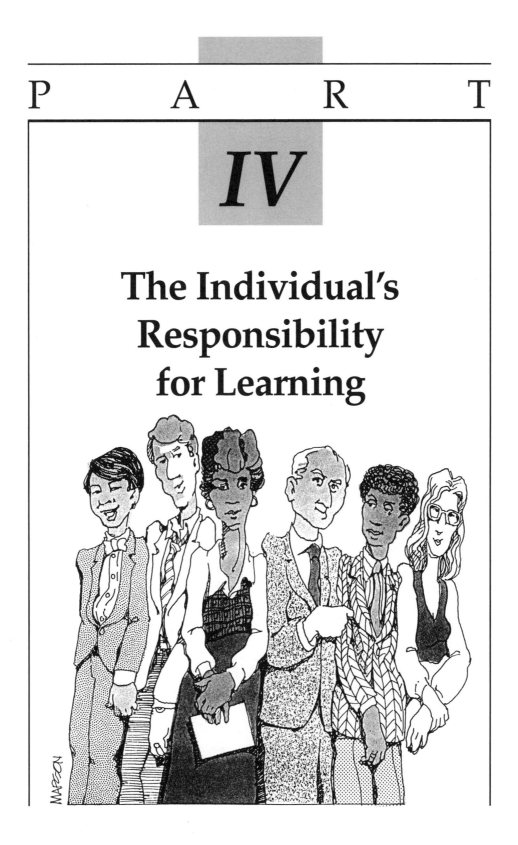

ATTITUDES TO CULTIVATE IN INDIVIDUAL LEARNERS

In any organization there are three types of learners. These types can be placed on a continuum just as the organizational tools were in Part II. On the left end are reluctant learners, people whose learning took place in the past. On the right end are lifelong learners, people who look to the future and decide what they need to learn today. And in the middle are leisurely learners, people with a focus on the present: "What do I need to learn right now to do my job?"

Read the following descriptions of each type of learner, and decide which type of learner you are.

RELUCTANT LEARNERS
Motto: Been There, Done That

- Resist learning anything new

- Regardless of education level, they feel they've already been to school

- Cling to the security of what they know

- See no need for further learning

- Live by phrases such as, "Can't teach an old dog new tricks"

- Whine that they don't get promoted

- Don't get the interesting assignments

- Are the first ones laid off when there is a downsizing.

In a class or a training program, these are the people sitting in the back of the classroom, rolling their eyes, and talking to their neighbors or working on something other than the course work. Reluctant learners can be a liability to your organization. Some may have been with the company for ten years, yet have gained only one year of experience ten times over.

ATTITUDES TO CULTIVATE IN INDIVIDUAL LEARNERS (continued)

LEISURELY LEARNERS
Motto: This Too Shall Pass

- Keep up with the required training to meet current expectations

- And that's about all they do, the minimum expected

- Sometimes complain, other times enjoy learning

- Don't volunteer for new assignments or ask to attend training programs

- Do what is recommended or required by their boss

- See teams as an opportunity to sit back and relax

- Many are successful because they know how to play the political games

In today's environment, they feel threatened and genuinely confused about all the changing expectations. The leisurely learner may become a reluctant learner if he or she is punished for learning, discouraged from learning, or encounters other organizational barriers to learning.

LIFELONG LEARNERS
Motto: If It's New, Try It

- Volunteer to attend learning events

- Read relevant books and professional magazines

- Talk with lots of people about what they're doing and how they're learning

- Watch for and anticipate the trends

- Prepare themselves to leap into the future

- Experiment with new ideas

Lifelong learners may have years of experience and be highly respected by their colleagues, yet they're always taking notes and drinking in new ideas. These are the people you want to cultivate and nurture in your organization.

In reality, we are all a little of each type of learner *in some area.* Each of us has a primary learning attitude, but with a little reflection, you can probably identify some area of learning that is not your main learning style. After reading the previous descriptions of learning attitudes, you have probably identified your basic attitude toward learning. Now work through the following exercise to identify areas of learning that may not be your main style.

EXERCISE: Learning Styles Identification

On the continuum below, list at least five examples for each category of learning attitude: These can be personal- or work-related areas. What are you reluctant to learn? What do you learn because it's required? What are you learning to prepare yourself for the future? To get you started, a few examples are listed.

PAST	PRESENT	FUTURE
← RELUCTANT	LEISURELY	LIFELONG →
Operate new equipment	Learn new software	Hobby
New exercise regimen	Time management techniques	Management skills

In some areas your attitude is that of a lifelong learner, while in other areas you are a reluctant learner. What seems to make the difference? We will explore this question in the later section, "How to Leverage Your Natural Desire to Learn."

Now let's take a look at what sets Lifelong Learners apart from the rest. The first difference is their attitude about mistakes.

LIFELONG LEARNERS FOLLOW UP ON THEIR MISTAKES

What do you do when you make a mistake? You have many choices of how to respond. Read through the following simple example and examine the different possibilities listed for responding to this error. Check the ones you would have used in the past.

You have just introduced the guest speaker at your company's annual meeting. Afterward, the speaker tells you that you mispronounced her name. What is your response?

☐ 1. "I said it right."

☐ 2. "The paper didn't say how to pronounce it."

☐ 3. "I said it the way you told me to."

☐ 4. "I didn't think anyone would notice."

☐ 5. "Oh, how *do* you pronounce your name?"

Now let's see what each of these responses represents.

► Statement #1 is an example of *denial.* In this case no learning takes place and you've created a potential conflict with the speaker.

► Statement #2 is an example of *defensiveness.* You have read a written, prepared introduction that didn't specify the pronunciation, so how can it be your fault? Still no learning takes place here, either.

► Statement #3 is an example of *blaming others* when a mistake is made. In this case, you've *certainly* aroused defensiveness in the speaker. Still no learning occurs.

► Statement #4 is an example of *trying to conceal* your mistake. You have erroneously assumed that if no one knows about it, it didn't really happen. Again, no learning occurs.

► With statement #5 there is an acknowledgment of the mistake and a statement of the desire to learn. A mistake is a trigger for learning—without making mistakes, you're just playing it safe and not growing or risking anything.

LIFELONG LEARNERS FOLLOW UP ON THEIR MISTAKES (continued)

What is your typical reaction when you make a mistake?

_____

_____

_____

_____

_____

Equally important, how do you respond when a mistake is made by someone else? Do you blame? Judge? Criticize? Or do you help the other person learn from the mistake?

_____

_____

_____

_____

_____

In many organizations mistakes are concealed because the consequence for making one is so negative. How does your organization treat a person who makes a mistake?

_____

_____

_____

_____

THE STAGES OF LEARNING

The Lifelong Learner isn't afraid to use these three magic words: **I don't know.** To people who want to learn, these words are empowering. If they don't know the answer, they can ask questions and seek out the answer. Too often, people are reluctant to use the magic words, fearing that they will be perceived as inadequate or incompetent.

Stage 1: Unconscious Incompetent

As you learn, you pass through stages of competence, as identified by William Howell in his book *Empathic Communications*. The first stage is *unconscious incompetent*. At this stage you don't know that you don't know, as in the expression, "what you don't know won't hurt you." In some respects this is a naive and blissful state, because there is no discomfort about not knowing something. For example, consider the manager who has just taken a job in a new company. She knows from the interview that the company is immersed in implementing a quality program, but she's never been exposed to what this means in day-to-day work. She's always tried to do quality work and can't imagine that this will be much different. This manager is an unconscious incompetent, knowing nothing of what will be required of her in her new job.

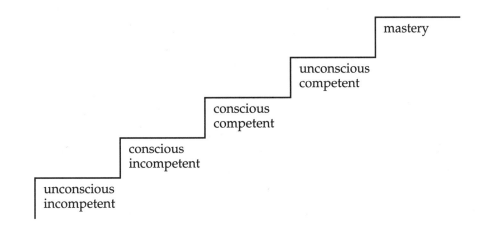

THE STAGES OF LEARNING (continued)

Stage 2: Conscious Incompetent

It doesn't take long for the new manager to move to the second stage: *conscious incompetent.* At this point, she *knows* she doesn't know. This is a time characterized by stress, sometimes disillusionment, and a significant opportunity to use the three magic words: I don't know. She's moved from the blissful ignorance state to a state of discomfort (at times extreme discomfort!). Now the manager is on the so-called *learning curve.* When she attends meetings, people talk about opportunity analysis, cause and effect matrix, and PERT charts. She is acutely aware that she doesn't know what these words mean, or how to use these quality tools. Her early attempts to apply the tools result in confusion and frustration.

Stage 3: Conscious Competent

As the weeks pass, the manager asks questions, practices using the quality tools and gradually achieves the stage of *conscious competent.* She begins to understand which tools to use in which situations. She knows how to use each of the tools effectively. She stops worrying that she'll embarass herself in a meeting because she doesn't know the difference between a PERT chart and a Gantt chart. At this stage, using the tools still demands concentration. But there is less stress, more fun, and a growing sense of pride in her new knowledge and skills. Discomfort begins its transformation into comfort.

Stage 4: Unconscious Competent

Continued practice gets the learner to the fourth stage: *unconscious competent.* At this point the manager no longer needs to check a reference manual for how to use a specific quality tool. She doesn't need to analyze which tool to use in a given situation. Using the tools has become enjoyable. What a wonderful place to reach! The skill has not only become familiar; it has become a reflex action.

But there are risks to this stage of unconscious competence.

Risk #1: Learning Arrogance

When you've worked diligently to learn a skill and practiced long and hard to become efficient at it, you are more likely to resist new ways of accomplishing that task. For instance, our manager is visited by a vendor one day, who suggests that there is a special computer and software package that will enable a team to make faster, wiser decisions. The vendor is convinced that the new technology is an advance over the quality tools the manager currently uses. But the manager is comfortable with her quality tools. Whether objections to innovation are verbalized or not, the message conveyed is, "My way is best." When the unconscious competent is experiencing success with one way, she may not be open to another way. Have you ever seen this happen?

Risk #2: Boredom

When you can do the job without thinking about it, where is the challenge? Where is the excitement? Ironically, a person at this advanced stage of learning can become a liability for an organization because she loses some motivation, has time to complain, and may resist new ways of doing things.

What's the solution to the pitfalls of unconscious competence? One answer is to begin a learning cycle again in a new area, or with a new skill. This is one of the benefits of job rotation and cross-training. Learners reenter the unconscious incompetent stage, which invites ongoing learning. Another solution is proposed by Bob Pike in his book, *Creative Training Techniques Handbook.* He suggests there is a fifth stage—conscious unconscious competent—which involves teaching others how to do what you do. This, of course, is one of the reasons learning organizations begin using internal trainers instead of relying only on the training department or outside experts. Teaching is one of the quickest ways to learn. Everyone can become a mentor in some area, which strengthens teamwork and cooperation.

THE STAGES OF LEARNING (continued)

Stage 5: Mastery

There is yet another stage of learning: *mastery*. George Leonard, author of *Mastery*, says that as a person learns, there are spurts of growth followed by a plateau. Early in the learning process, the spurts of growth are closer together and there's a sense of accomplishment. However, the time spent on the plateau grows longer as the climb becomes steeper and the refinements more subtle. Leonard uses aikido, a Japanese martial art based on joint locks and throws, as his analogy. Many people begin a martial art and enjoy the first year or so of classes when learning is most rapid. But then they stop coming to classes. They never earn their black belt. That's because most people, particularly in Western cultures, enjoy the feeling that is associated with the growth spurt. They start new projects and experience that initial thrill of learning and accomplishment. But as soon as the learning slows down and becomes more subtle, they tire of the project and turn their attention to something new. People often don't stay with one thing long enough to truly master it.

Think of each of the learning stages as a plateau. Some people won't stick with learning something long enough to master it, to reach that sixth stage. Mastery is a process and not an endpoint to be reached. The challenge is to learn to love the plateau since that is where you spend the bulk of your life.

The growth spurts are peaks, moments that are not sustained. They motivate you to continue practicing on the plateau, knowing that eventually you'll move from this plateau to another.

The process of mastering something requires both time and commitment. A meditation teacher once said, "If you insist on evaluating your practice, do it only at 10-year intervals." Yet we want our companies to show profits and growth on a quarterly basis! That short-term mind-set is in direct contradiction to the process of learning. Mastery as an approach to learning and running our organizations represents transformation—another paradigm shift.

Examining Your Own Learned Skills

Take a few minutes now to apply these concepts to your work life. Think of something that you've learned and have taken from the stage of unconscious incompetence toward mastery.

What are examples of skills that you've developed as far as conscious competence?

_____

_____

_____

Give an example of a skill that you are now teaching to others (mentoring).

_____

_____

_____

What are you currently practicing that you would like to master?

_____

_____

_____

OPENNESS TO LEARNING

The Lifelong Learner keeps an open mind to learning. It is a significant accomplishment to do this and avoid learning arrogance and the tendency to judge. How does one stay open? Here are some tips.

► **Surrender**

At its simplest, this is acknowledging that you don't know. You surrender to the teacher, to the process or to the task to learn. Surrender can happen at first learnings, when something is brand new, and it can happen when you're well on the way toward mastery.

► **Be Curious**

This is a state common to children, especially young children, in which the world is filled with wonder. As a learner, you want to understand and experience the wonder. This feeling state takes you outside of yourself, and focuses you on the object or subject about which you feel curious.

► **Have Intent or Purpose**

Approach life with an intention to learn. Believe that part of your purpose in each activity, interaction or experience is to learn. Closely aligned with intent is the decision to act on the intent.

► **Suspend Expectations**

When you want to learn something, it is easy to slip away from intending to learn, to an expectation of how fast you'll learn or how easy it will be. Lifelong Learners allow the learning to unfold over time, not according to a predetermined schedule.

► **Look the Fool**

A true learner is willing to be clumsy or awkward at first. Try to understand the paradox, "If it's worth doing well, it's worth doing poorly." In other words, you will make mistakes in the beginning (you'll do poorly) at what you intend to master (what's worth doing well). Learning can be untidy and you may look foolish as you learn, but the Lifelong Learner values each step along the way.

► **Ask Questions**

When you're a Lifelong Learner, you are willing to expose the fact that you don't know. Your openness to learning is expressed by your willingness to ask questions, even at the risk that others will think the question is "dumb." The Lifelong Learner recognizes, as did Socrates, that questions stimulate learning. Challenge yourself to ask ten questions about everything you want to learn.

► Be Humble

This principle is captured well in the phrase, "The more I learn, the less I know." Accept your not knowing as normal. The Lifelong Learner doesn't expect to know all there is to know about everything. *Not* to know is the more common state of affairs—especially when you consider that 50,000 new books are released each year, and the amount of available information doubles every three years.

► Seek the Truth

At heart, Lifelong Learners want to know the truth. In pursuit of that truth, they stay open to all learning. Truth is understood as something we can only approximate with our current knowledge and experience. To reach truth is a task of a lifetime.

► Be Ready and Patient

Be kind to yourself as you learn. Sometimes the timing is just not right. "To everything there is a season," and learning is no exception. Practice recognizing the difference between your resistance and readiness. A tulip doesn't resist blooming in the winter, it is simply waiting for its time in the spring. Be sensitive to the building blocks that need to be in place before you can learn a skill or something about yourself.

CHECKLIST: *Identify Blocks to Openness*

Just as there are qualities that enable you to open the door to learning, there are qualities that shut that door. Read through this list and check the blocks to openness that you are aware are impairing your learning process.

☐ "I want to look good to protect my self-esteem."

☐ "I tend to be a 'know-it-all.' "

☐ "I can never figure things out on my own."

☐ "That method just won't work."

☐ "That teacher/instructor isn't doing a good job/isn't explaining things right."

☐ "I don't trust myself to retain this knowledge."

☐ "Others won't respect me if I don't know everything."

☐ "I have to be perfect."

☐ "I couldn't learn it before, and I can't now either."

☐ "My way is best, no matter what."

RISK TAKING

Inherent in most learning is taking risks. At any learning moment, there is the risk of looking the fool, which we have discussed. There is also a risk associated with changing your behavior. You risk shaking up your current beliefs and values when you learn. You take a chance of making mistakes. You put your current level of competence on the line to try doing something in a new way, in which you aren't yet competent. The list of risks is a long one.

More important than our list of risks, however, is your list. From your own perspective, what do you risk when you put yourself into a learning situation?

_____

_____

_____

_____

_____

_____

How Do You Feel About Taking Risks?

Because learning and risk taking are so closely associated, it's important to take time to reflect on your own personal risk-taking behavior. Life is certainly not linear, but for now, imagine your life to be like the line on page 81. At the left end of the life-line is birth, and at the right end is death.

A sample life-line has been completed to get you started. Above the life-line, write the risks that you have taken in your life. This part of the exercise is relatively easy for most people. The more difficult part is writing down the risks that you *didn't* take, below the life-line. You will need a period of quiet reflection to get in touch with the risks you haven't taken. To get the maximum learning from this exercise, give yourself 30 minutes to complete both parts.

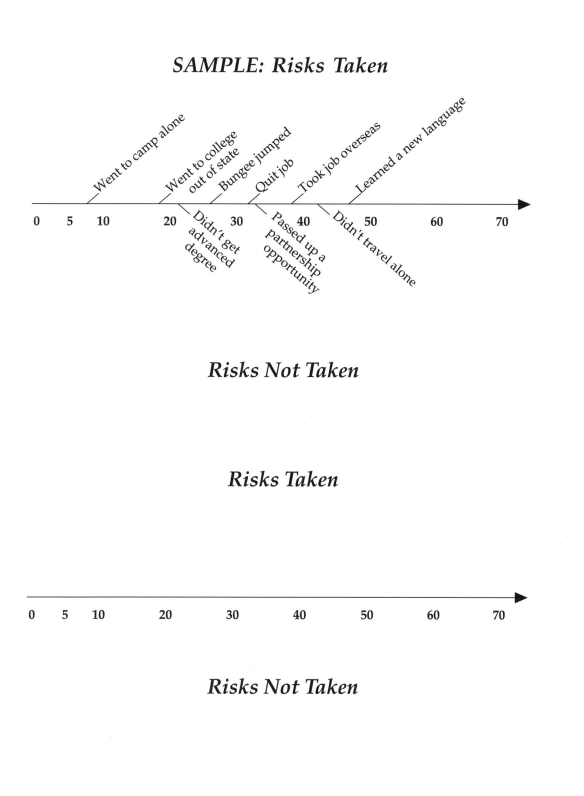

SAMPLE: *Risks Taken*

Risks Not Taken

Risks Taken

Risks Not Taken

RISK TAKING (continued)

After completing your personal risk life-line, answer these questions:

1. What have you learned about yourself through the risks you've taken?

_____

_____

2. When do you tend to take risks?

_____

_____

3. At moments of choice, do you tend to move toward learning (growth), or to maintaining the status quo?

_____

_____

4. What have been the outcomes of the risks you've taken?

_____

_____

5. What have been the outcomes of the risks you haven't taken?

_____

_____

6. What relationship do you observe between your willingness to take risks and your perception of yourself as a Reluctant, Leisurely or Lifelong Learner?

_____

_____

YOUR PERSONAL RESPONSIBILITY FOR LEARNING

No one can make you learn. No one but you is responsible for your learning. If you happen to feel bored in your current job, that is not someone else's fault. The boredom is *your personal responsibility*. There are things you can do, already outlined in this book, to ease the boredom. It is not the responsibility of your organization or your bosses to make your work stimulating and meaningful.

Learning means applying what you know, and changing your behavior based on what you discover. No one can do this for you. Anyone can tell you the secrets of good health, or success, or how to be happy, but only you can apply that knowledge to your life. In the application is the learning.

So if you've been blaming others, the time to stop is *now.* It's time to grow up and take responsibility for yourself, your life and what you're getting out of it. If you don't like the results you're getting, try something new. And if you don't like the way information is presented to you, take responsibility for telling people how you learn best. (You'll find more about this subject in the later section, "The Seven Intelligences.")

For the person who takes responsibility for his own learning, regardless of what support the organization may provide, there are two benefits: First, he receives the joy and pleasure that are intrinsic to learning. Second, what he's learned can never be taken away. If your organization doesn't acknowledge or reward learning, be ready to find one that does!

Leslie Charles, President of Trainingworks, suggests any person can use a *learning log* to support her own learning. Each day, choose one behavior you want to practice, and write it down in a notebook. At the end of the day, make notes on your progress. This simple learning log will help you make learning a conscious choice each day. Here are some examples of learning goals: Maintain a positive attitude; pay attention to how I use my body at the computer; smile more.

In addition to using a learning log for your own learning, you can share it with people in your organization. What would you like to focus on learning today? To help yourself get started, complete the following sentences:

I want to learn more about _____

I want to practice _____

I want to research _____

YOUR PERSONAL RESPONSIBILITY FOR LEARNING (continued)

Corporate trainers, presidents, CEOs and others directly concerned about transforming an organization into a learning organization need to remember that each person in the company will make a personal choice about his learning. Not everyone will be a Lifelong Learner. Leisurely Learners have the potential to become Lifelong Learners if they observe that learning is rewarded. Reluctant Learners can be helped to find a place outside of the organization, where perhaps they will become Leisurely or Lifelong Learners.

Discovery vs. Judgment

Dana Gribben, a speech coach in San Francisco, teaches a very important lesson about judgment:

"When you judge, you aren't participating anymore."

Think about that for a moment. Judgment prevents learning. When you judge, you're engaged in a closed-loop interaction with yourself. For example, have you ever attended a training program and along the way thought to yourself, "What a silly exercise," or perhaps, "This is so basic, I bet I've done this exercise a dozen times!" At that moment you are not doing the exercise. You are not participating and you are not learning. You've removed yourself from what is really happening. As long as you're judging, you can't be learning.

So what can you do to counteract the tendency to judgment that comes quickly and easily to most of us? Most of just judge so often that we aren't even aware of it. We may judge ourselves, others or a situation. The first step is to catch yourself in the middle of judgment. Then, trade in your judgment for *discovery*.

Discovery is an attitude that keeps you open to learning. Don't try to decide if you like or dislike, agree or disagree. Simply look to see what is. Explore it. The discoveries you make may be about yourself, the situation or the specific content or skill that you're learning. With this attitude of discovery, there is something to be learned in any situation.

CREATIVE OR REACTIVE/ RESPONSIVE?

Robert Fritz, in his book *The Path of Least Resistance,* laid out two alternative ways to live life. He calls one orientation *the creative,* and the other orientation *reactive-responsive.*

Most people live from the orientation of the reactive-responsive. In that orientation, you react to what life gives you. You respond to the situations in which you find yourself. Consequently, you often feel powerless to control your life or its events. "Some people have all the luck," you think. Their lives apparently flow, while you're stuck with bad luck and lousy breaks. That is not an empowering way to live your life. If this is your orientation to life, most of your learning is probably accidental and retrospective.

In sharp contrast, from the orientation of the creative, you are empowered to decide what *you* want out of life. Using the tools Fritz outlines in his book, you can go about the process of creating the outcomes you want, proactively deciding what you want to learn in your life and not leaving it to chance. Lifelong Learners live from the orientation of the creative.

WORKING THROUGH CREATIVE TENSION

At the core of the orientation of the creative is the task of managing the *creative tension* between your current reality and your vision of what you want. As shown in the following graphic, you start with a vision, something you want to create in your life. Think now about something you want to learn. Describe it as clearly and vividly as you can, so that you know you'll recognize it when you get it. Then tell yourself the truth about your current reality. What is your situation right now? Include in your description of current reality any feelings you have about where you are in relation to your goal. The gap between your vision and current reality is called creative tension.

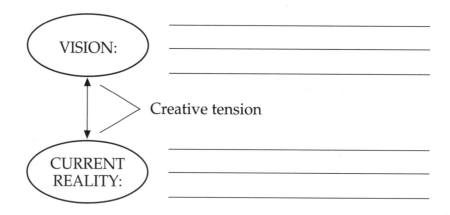

There are two ways to resolve creative tension. One is to drop the vision. In this way the tension is eliminated. Of course, if this is your way of resolving the tension, your self-respect and esteem will also suffer a blow. The second way to resolve the tension is to bring your current reality into alignment with your vision. That technique is the way of the orientation of the creative. It's also the way of the Lifelong Learner.

CASE STUDY: *Using Creative Tension*

Here's an example of using the orientation of the creative in real life. Your author travels a good deal, and decided she wanted to feel safe when out alone. She also wanted to become physically fit. That was her vision. Learning the martial art aikido seemed an excellent way to achieve both of these goals. Her current reality was that she had no experience with a martial art and was afraid of being thrown. Nor had she ever participated in a regular, ongoing exercise program. The gap between where she was (unskilled and untoned) and where she wanted to be (strong and competent) was the creative tension.

Over years of practice there were many times when getting to class was difficult; when she didn't want to do what was necessary to reach the vision. As motivation, she asked herself a simple question: Do I still want the vision? The answer was yes. However, she still wanted to stay home sometimes, spend time with family or read a good book. Those feelings became part of her current reality. There were many times when she drove to the dojo (the place of practice) thinking, "I don't want to go."

Dropping the goal would be the easier path. But she still wants the goal, and holds the same vision. Until she achieves that vision, a gap will exist between the current reality and the goal. In the meantime, however, she'll be able to see how current reality has advanced toward the vision.

As you work to transform your company into a learning organization, remember that the gap between where you are and where you want to be is the very fuel that will enable you to reach your vision. The orientation of the creative allows you to concentrate less on problems, and more on challenges.

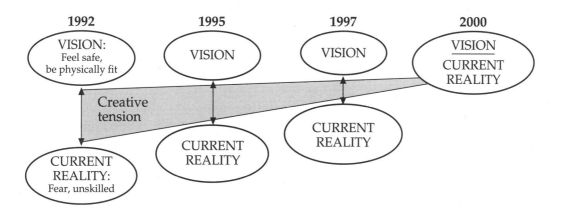

LEVERAGING THE NATURAL DESIRE TO LEARN

It's a well-known motivation principle that people do things for their own reasons, not for someone else's reasons. This principle applies just as clearly to learning. The more you understand what is behind someone's desire to learn, the more you can support them in their learning. In the process, you'll leverage the learning that's occurring overall in your organization. Let's examine some motivations to learn.

✓ **Curiosity.**

We've talked about this as a natural drive toward learning that exists in human beings at birth. That innate curiosity has been encouraged to a greater or lesser degree in all of us. Some people in your organization will want to learn about everything, and their motive is pure and simple: curiosity.

✓ **Self-protection.**

In our rapidly changing environment, many people realize that to keep their job, they must continuously develop new skills. Consequently, some people will take courses, seek out mentors, and maximize other learning opportunities not because they see intrinsic value in learning, but because they want to insulate themselves against change. This type of learning is motivated by fear.

✓ **To fulfill a purpose.**

Some people come to work for something to do, but many are there because they want to do something. They'd like to touch lives and make a difference. For them, work is a passion or a calling. Listening to this inner call, they are motivated to learn whatever will bring them into closer alignment with their purpose as they see it.

✓ **Reward or profit.**

Certainly there are people who are motivated by financial gain. And in some fields, the more you learn, the more you earn. In professions such as social work, psychology and accounting, a person who achieves certification or licensure will command a higher salary. Some companies base their pay scale in part upon the number of courses taken and successfully completed, or may grant jobs and promotions when certain courses or educational requirements are met. Thus, some people are motivated to learn because of a tangible reward.

✓ Through painful or negative experiences.

Anyone who has been in the workforce for a number of years has probably at some time worked with a difficult or ineffective boss. This apparently negative experience can actually be a profound learning experience. By observing the behaviors of the difficult person, you learn how *not* to behave. You discover that the way you are being managed is different from the way you want to be managed. This is an outstanding example of the advantage given by an attitude of discovery; being nonjudgmental can turn a painful experience into insight and growth.

✓ Fun.

Learning can indeed be fun. Everyone needs a little play in their lives, and learning can be a way to have that. Increasingly, games are a part of learning programs, and laughter comes out of boardrooms and class-rooms everywhere. The most effective foreign-language program in the world, according to *The Learning Revolution* by Dryden and Vos, is from Accelerated Learning Systems in England. It combines music, stories, and play acting into a highly successful program that is fun and effective. Children learn through play, so why not adults?

✓ When expectations aren't met.

Suppose you're chairing a meeting and you don't get through the agenda in the time allowed. You may feel discomfort because *your expectations haven't been met.* This is a powerful motivator for learning. When expectations aren't met, there's an opportunity to set the orien-tation of the creative in motion. If you want your next meeting to run more smoothly, you'll want to learn how to plan an agenda. You have a goal, current reality doesn't match the goal, and so you'll make an effort to bring the two into alignment through learning.

✓ For future focus.

People who work in a rapidly developing field or industry and want to stay in that industry five years or so from today must invest learning time *now* if they want to be a real part of that future. For example, in professional speaking and training, multimedia presentations will be the standard visual aid of the future. The motivation to learn about graphics, LCD panels and other projection devices is thus directly inspired by a desire to remain in the field in the future.

LEVERAGING THE NATURAL DESIRE TO LEARN (continued)

✓ It's mandatory.

Requiring training is another way to motivate through fear. Whenever a particular training session or skill is made *mandatory*, people look for what the consequence will be if they don't learn. Depending upon the perceived severity of the consequence, obligation may or may not motivate. This strategy reflects the control imposed by hierarchical organizations of the past, and will be of decreasing use in the new learning organization. Because certain programs are required by law, this motivator may never disappear completely, however.

✓ Enjoyment.

Some people simply love learning! Learning is a pleasure in and of itself. It leads to self-esteem and confidence. It energizes and stimulates the person—a true natural high.

In addition to these ten motivators for learning, there may be others that you would like to include. It's important for each learner, yourself included, to know why and when he or she is most likely to learn. Now that we've examined the why, let's take a look at the when. To uncover this for yourself, begin by describing three significant learning experiences in your life. These may be job related or personal.

Learning Experience #1: _____

_____

Learning Experience #2: _____

_____

Learning Experience #3: _____

_____

Reflect on these three learning experiences and ask yourself what motivated you to learn. Was it the same motivator in each situation? Were there several reasons you learned in that situation? Did something motivate you that wasn't on the list you just studied?

THE SEVEN INTELLIGENCES

Howard Gardner, in his book *Frames of Mind,* identifies seven different *intelligences.* Most people are only aware of the ones that are typically emphasized in school, such as math and language. Discovering all the other intelligences changes an individual's self-perception, and opens them to learning what they may have previously avoided.

Lifelong Learners know their strengths and try to leverage them. As you read through the seven intelligences, put a checkmark beside the ones that you think are strongest for you. What is the relationship between your intelligences and what you prefer to learn? Is there a relationship between what you resist learning and your weakest intelligences?

☐ **#1 Musical**

This intelligence emerges before any other and is not highly valued in North American culture. If musical aptitude is one of your preferred intelligences, you're aware that you carry sounds in your head. Composers have this intelligence, and it uses primarily the auditory channel.

☐ **#2 Linguistic**

Unlike musical intelligence, linguistic intelligence emerges more slowly and often does not peak until age 50, 60 or even 70. That's why many writers do their best work in their later years. Poets, writers and people who love the sound of words and their shades of meaning have this intelligence. Reading, writing and communicating with words comes from this intelligence. Linguistic intelligence is highly valued in school. Like music, it uses the auditory channel as well.

☐ **#3 Logical/Mathematical**

Scientists, lawyers and mathematicians have this intelligence. It begins with objects to be counted and becomes quite abstract. In fact, the reasoning of a person with logical/mathematical intelligence can become so complex that the average person has trouble understanding. Chess players have this intelligence. It peaks early, usually by age 30 to 40, and also arrives early, as does musical intelligence. Logical/mathematical intelligence is the other aptitude highly valued in school.

☐ **#4 Spatial**

Like logical/mathematical intelligence, spatial intelligence is involved with objects—recognizing them in different elements or when they've been transformed. This is the intelligence of the graphic artist, architect, navigator and pilot. It does not deteriorate with age and is "right brain" oriented.

THE SEVEN INTELLIGENCES (continued)

☐ **#5 Body/Kinesthetic**

People with this intelligence use their bodies in a controlled way. Dancers, mimes, martial artists and athletes have body/kinesthetic intelligence. They can skillfully handle objects and develop mechanical skills.

☐ **#6 Intrapersonal**

This intelligence varies by culture, but the focus is on the inner life, feelings and intuitions. Spiritual teachers and religious leaders have this intrapersonal intelligence. Introspection is part of this intelligence, as well.

☐ **#7 Interpersonal**

This intelligence, too, is influenced by your culture. It has an outward focus, involving relationships, detecting the feelings of others, and knowing oneself in relation to others. Salespeople and motivators have this intelligence.

7 Intelligences

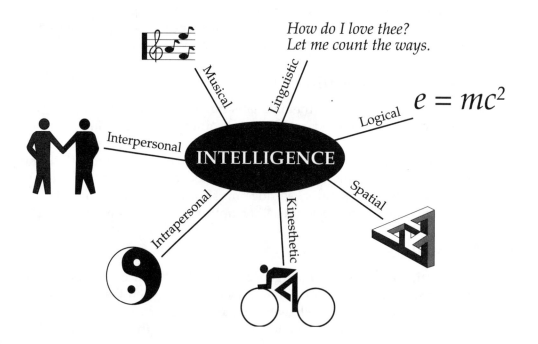

How do I love thee?
Let me count the ways.

$e = mc^2$

Musical · Linguistic · Logical · Interpersonal · INTELLIGENCE · Spatial · Intrapersonal · Kinesthetic

TELL YOURSELF THE TRUTH ABOUT CURRENT REALITY

An important part of the orientation of the creative is to tell yourself the truth about current reality. If your vision is to become a Lifelong Learner or to help someone else become one, then you need to honestly and accurately describe where you are right now. Though you may start out awkward, uncertain or scared, there is no need to judge your current reality. It is what it is. The more you know about it, the better you can plan to close the gap between it and your vision.

As an aspiring Lifelong Learner, describe in a paragraph your current reality.

_____

_____

_____

_____

_____

_____

Use the same process to describe your organization. Assuming the vision is to create a learning organization, what is the current reality of your company?

_____

_____

_____

_____

_____

_____

What follows on page 94 is a list of some typical components of current reality. Do any of these sound like yours or your organization's?

TELL YOURSELF THE TRUTH ABOUT CURRENT REALITY (continued)

I'm Too Busy

If you have a report due on Friday, how can you possibly be expected to commit a day to a training program? If you have a budget to prepare, why do you have to spend time reflecting on the effectiveness of a staff meeting? When there's a deadline to meet, how do you make time to practice a new communication model with a co-worker?

These are real concerns and challenges for someone becoming a Lifelong Learner and for a group becoming a learning organization. The critical issue is, what do you value? To what do you aspire? If learning is integrated into who you are and the way you work, it is no longer something that's outside your mainstream job activities. Learning *is* your job. Time invested in learning today saves time tomorrow.

Fear

By definition, when you're learning, you're on your growing edge. Depending upon the type of learning you're engaged in, you will experience more or less fear associated with it. For example, if you're in incremental learning (how to use a new feature of a computer program you already use, for instance), there will be less fear than if you're making a paradigm shift to a new procedure for getting the work done.

Looking more deeply into the issue, what is it that you fear? Often you are afraid that you won't "get it." The learning will be too difficult, and you'll look stupid. You'll be left behind your peers. These are issues of self-esteem.

You may also fear that the learning won't be applied. Why invest the time, especially when you're so busy, just to find out it was wasted time because the new method won't be implemented? Or perhaps the fear is that you'll discover something about yourself that you don't really want to know. Or you might need to change your patterns with new learning.

The most effective response to fear is to acknowledge it, name it, and move forward toward your vision. Don't make the mistake of letting fear give you the message, "Don't do it."

What other reasons can you think of for a person being afraid to learn?

_____

_____

_____

Weak Follow-Through

It's critical to remember that learning is not the same thing as knowing. Learning takes place when behavior changes. You may "know" that exercise is good for you, but until you "do" an exercise program, true learning hasn't taken place. You can "know" that communication is enhanced when you practice reflective listening, but the learning of that habit takes place in the day-to-day, unconsciously competent application of what you know.

Too often we gain knowledge and feel convinced about the benefits of applying the knowledge to our lives. Then, when it comes to the follow-through of implementing what we know, we get sloppy. With weak follow-through, the result is less learning than is otherwise possible.

What is the secret, then, to applying learning? There is no secret. You need to decide to apply what you know. Until you make learning a priority, it will happen only by accident.

Lack of Vision

In a learning project for a branch of state government, the training facilitator met with each top manager for an individual consultation around his or her learning goals for the coming year. One manager, in her job for 15 years, said, "There's nothing I want to learn. I like my job and I only have 17 years until I retire." This person had no vision for herself. She was content at the moment and could seen no value in learning. In further discussions, she went on to say she knew her job very well and there wasn't anything new to learn.

Unfortunately, some people drift into learning arrogance, living from the orientation of reactive-responsive. When they realize their skills haven't kept up with the new ways of doing things, it may be too late to catch up.

TELL YOURSELF THE TRUTH ABOUT CURRENT REALITY (continued)

No matter what your current station in life, there is always something to be learned. Take control of your life and decide what you want to learn.

Lack of Personal Resources

It's not uncommon to want to pursue an academic degree and be blocked by inadequate financial resources or substantial family time commitments. Or perhaps you are put off by the discovery that you don't have a "natural gift" for a skill that you want to learn.

Most of these barriers can be overcome; however, it may not happen on your personal time schedule. The degree may need to wait until your children are older. An acting career may have to become an avocation rather than a vocation. Use your creativity and the mentors in your life to strategize ways of responding to insufficient personal resources.

Low Self-Esteem

Self-esteem is how you feel about yourself. When you like yourself, you're more apt to have self-confidence and to trust yourself. Without self-esteem it's hard to believe in yourself. Without self-confidence you may be more hesitant about learning opportunities, to doubt your ability to accomplish something. This negative self-talk will kill your desire to learn.

If you experience feelings of low self-esteem, self-doubt, or worthlessness, your first learning assignment is to build up your esteem. One critical tool is building success experiences of "I can . . ." Get started today!

Judgment

When you're not "getting it," when you feel uncomfortable, when you can't see the purpose of something—that's when it's easy to quiet your discomfort with a negative judgment.

"This is dumb, who needs it anyway!?"

"What does he know about my job? Maybe his ideas work for marketing, but they'll never work for me."

"I wish I had half the money this company wastes on training courses."

"If they'd leave me alone and let me do my job, everything would be fine."

Whether your judgment is directed at yourself or outside yourself, that judgment shuts down your ability to learn and damages your self-esteem. Try to catch yourself as you're in the midst of a judgment. Then simply name what you are doing. "Oh, I'm judging." Do not criticize yourself for judging, either. Saying something like, "There I go again judging. I make no progress. What's wrong with me anyway?" doesn't solve anything. Stick to a simple naming of what you are doing. Then refocus your attention on the learning task at hand. This skill in handling judgment as you learn can be applied to all areas of your life, with dramatic results. You'll increase self-esteem, develop inner calm, and reduce stress. Try it.

FIVE STRATEGIES TO MANAGE CREATIVE TENSION

You have a vision for yourself to become a lifelong learner, and you've told yourself the truth about current reality. Now how will you close the gap between the two? Jot down your ideas on the diagram below. Then check your ideas against those presented in this section.

How I'll Close the Gap:

_____

_____

_____

Here's an acronym to help you remember the key strategies for managing creative tension, which is the gap between your vision and current reality. Take PRIDE with you whenever you want to learn!

P----------- **P**eople

R ---------- **R**esearch, read

I ----------- **I**ntrospection

D ---------- **D**o

E----------- obs**E**rve

Here are examples of each of these tools to get you started.

People

- Ask questions
- Seek out a mentor
- Listen to what people say in meetings
- Network
- Join and participate in professional associations
- Pick up the phone and call someone
- Talk to people

Research, read

- Subscribe to relevant journals
- Go to the library
- Read on a regular basis
- Subscribe to an online information service, such as America Online or CompuServe
- Learn to navigate the Internet
- Make friends with your local librarian
- Attend conferences, institutes, satellite trainings
- Seek exposure to cutting-edge ideas
- Frequent bookstores
- Read book reviews
- Subscribe to audio learning programs

FIVE STRATEGIES TO MANAGE CREATIVE TENSION (continued)

Introspection

- Take time to reflect
- Think through an action before you take it
- Study the way you handled yourself in a particular situation
- Analyze
- Look deeply into situations
- Question with an intent to understand rather than judge
- Keep a journal
- Write out your ideas as a concept or "white" paper

Do

- Try it
- Experiment
- Use trial and error
- Implement
- Throw yourself into the middle of the thing
- Get your hands dirty
- Take action—move your body, hands, feet
- Feel it in your body
- Take action
- Put your pen to paper and start writing
- Put your fingers on the keyboard and start typing
- Pick up the phone and dial
- Just do it

obs**E**rve

- Watch others
- Look for role models
- Pay attention
- Don't judge
- Seek to understand what you see
- Study facial expressions
- Examine behaviors
- Study how others handle situations
- Use all your senses

Remember that others are observing you as they learn. Are you modeling the behaviors of a Lifelong Learner?

The power in your learning comes when you can integrate all five of these PRIDE strategies. Remember them by letting each one be represented by a finger on your hand. The easiest way to open a door is to push it with all five fingers. Let PRIDE open your doors to learning.

FIVE STRATEGIES TO MANAGE CREATIVE TENSION (continued)

Recall a successful learning experience. Jot down a brief summary of it here.

_____

_____

Which of the five learning strategies did you use and how?

People _____

Research _____

Introspection _____

Doing _____

obs**E**rve _____

Of the five, which ones do you tend to use most often?

_____

Which one(s) do you use least often?

_____

What relationship do you notice between your preferred intelligences and your preferred learning strategies?

_____

_____

_____

_____

_____

_____

_____

SUMMARY

In a changing world, learning is one of the few competitive advantages. If *Creating a Learning Organization* has fulfilled its purpose, you now have the guidance you need to turn your organization into a learning organization.

The following poem, written by Portia Nelson and quoted in *The Tibetan Book of Living and Dying* by Sogyal Rinpoche, beautifully captures what we've all experienced in our learning at one time or another, whether as an individual or as an organization. If your organization has embarked upon the journey to become a learning organization you'll undoubtedly recognize your process in these lines. May this book help you "walk down another street."

Autobiography in Five Chapters

1) I walk down the street.
There is a deep hole in the sidewalk.
I fall in.
I am lost . . . I am hopeless.
It isn't my fault.
It takes forever to find a way out.

2) I walk down the same street.
There is a deep hole in the sidewalk.
I pretend I don't see it.
I fall in again.
I can't believe I'm in the same place.
But it isn't my fault.
It still takes a long time to get out.

3) I walk down the same street.
There is a deep hole in the sidewalk.
I see it is there.
I still fall in . . . it's a habit.
My eyes are open.
I know where I am.
It is *my* fault.
I get out immediately.

4) I walk down the same street.
There is a deep hole in the sidewalk.
I walk around it.

5) I walk down another street.

FOR MORE INFORMATION

Braham, Barbara. *Finding Your Purpose.* Menlo Park, California: Crisp, 1991.

Dryden, Gordon, and Jeanette Vos. *The Learning Revolution.* Rolling Hills Estates, California: Jalmar Press, 1994.

Ford, Susan. "You can teach an old dog new tricks," *Good People.* Employers Insurance of Wausau: Wausau, Wisconsin, November 1994: p. 5.

Fritz, Robert. *The Path of Least Resistance.* Salem, Massachusetts: DMA, Inc., 1984.

Gardner, Howard. *Frames of Mind.* New York: Basic Books Inc., 1985.

Hackett, Donald, and Charles Martin. *Facilitation Skills for Managers.* Menlo Park, California: Crisp, 1993.

Howell, William. *Empathic Communicator.* Belmont, California: Wadsworth, 1982.

Kelly, Kevin, with Peter Burrows. "Motorola: Training for the Millenium," *Businessweek,* March 28, 1994: p. 158–163.

LeBoeuf, Michael. *The Greatest Management Principle in the World.* New York: Berkley, 1989.

Leonard, George. *Mastery.* New York: Penguin, 1991.

Narisette, Raju. "Executive Suites' Walls Come Tumbling Down," *The Wall Street Journal,* June 29, 1994, p. B-1.

Pike, Robert. *Creative Training Techniques.* Minneapolis, Minnesota: Lakewood Books, 1989.

Rinpoche, Sogyal. *The Tibetan Book of Living and Dying.* New York: HarperSanFrancisco, 1992.

Scott, Cynthia, Dennis Jaffe, and Glenn Tobe. *Organizational Vision, Values and Mission.* Menlo Park, California: Crisp, 1993.

Senge, Peter. *The Fifth Descipline.* New York: Doubleday, 1990.

Shea, Gordon. *Mentoring.* Menlo Park, California: Crisp, 1992.

Steinbach, Bob. *The Adult Learner.* Menlo Park, California: Crisp, 1993.

Suzuki, Shunryu. *Zen Mind, Beginner's Mind.* New York: John Weatherhill, 1970.

Wick, Calhoun. *The Learning Edge.* New York: McGraw-Hill, 1993.

NOTES

NOTES

NOTES

NOTES

NOW AVAILABLE FROM
CRISP PUBLICATIONS

Books • Videos • CD Roms • Computer-Based Training Products

Subject Areas Include:

Management

Human Resources

Communication Skills

Personal Development

Marketing/Sales

Organizational Development

Customer Service/Quality

Computer Skills

Small Business and Entrepreneurship

Adult Literacy and Learning

Life Planning and Retirement

CRISP WORLDWIDE DISTRIBUTION

English language books are distributed worldwide. Major international distributors include:

ASIA/PACIFIC

Australia/New Zealand: In Learning, PO Box 1051, Springwood QLD, Brisbane, Australia 4127   Tel: 61-7-3-841-2286, Facsimile: 61-7-3-841-1580
ATTN: Messrs. Gordon

Singapore: 85, Genting Lane, Guan Hua Warehouse Bldng #05-01, Singapore 349569   Tel: 65-749-3389, Facsimile: 65-749-1129
ATTN: Evelyn Lee

Japan: Phoenix Associates Co., LTD., Mizuho Bldng. 3-F, 2-12-2, Kami Osaki, Shinagawa-Ku, Tokyo 141   Tel: 81-33-443-7231, Facsimile: 81-33-443-7640
ATTN: Mr. Peter Owans

CANADA

Reid Publishing, Ltd., Box 69559-109 Thomas Street, Oakville, Ontario Canada L6J 7R4.   Tel: (905) 842-4428, Facsimile: (905) 842-9327
ATTN: Mr. Stanley Reid

Trade Book Stores: *Raincoast Books,* 8680 Cambie Street, Vancouver, B.C., V6P 6M9   Tel: (604) 323-7100, Facsimile: (604) 323-2600
ATTN: Order Desk

EUROPEAN UNION

England: *Flex Training,* Ltd. 9-15 Hitchin Street, Baldock, Hertfordshire, SG7 6A, England   Tel: 44-1-46-289-6000, Facsimile: 44-1-46-289-2417
ATTN: Mr. David Willetts

INDIA

Multi-Media HRD, Pvt., Ltd., National House, Tulloch Road, Appolo Bunder, Bombay, India 400-039   Tel: 91-22-204-2281, Facsimile: 91-22-283-6478
ATTN: Messrs. Aggarwal

SOUTH AMERICA

Mexico: *Grupo Editorial Iberoamerica,* Nebraska 199, Col. Napoles, 03810 Mexico, D.F.   Tel: 525-523-0994, Facsimile: 525-543-1173
ATTN: Señor Nicholas Grepe

SOUTH AFRICA

Alternative Books, Unit A3 Micro Industrial Park, Hammer Avenue, Stridom Park, Randburg, 2194 South Africa   Tel: 27-11-792-7730, Facsimile: 27-11-792-7787
ATTN: Mr. Vernon de Haas